SCOTS-DUTCH LINKS IN EUROPE AND AMERICA 1575–1825

Volume III

ANCIENT ROYAL ARMS

OF THE

KINGDOM OF SCOTLAND.

Woodcut used by John Davidson, Printer, in " Actis
maid be James the Fift," Edinburgh, 1541.

SCOTS-DUTCH LINKS
IN EUROPE AND AMERICA
1575–1825

Volume III

By
David Dobson

CLEARFIELD

Printed for Clearfield Company by
Genealogical Publishing Company
Baltimore, Maryland
2016

ISBN 978-0-8063-5820-8

Made in the United States of America

INTRODUCTION

Scotland has had strong economic and social links with the Netherlands since the medieval period, but the main period of settlement in the Low Countries by Scots occurred in the seventeenth century, *'de gouden eeuw'* of the Dutch.

Scottish scholars and merchants had long been attracted by the opportunities available in the universities and cities of Holland, Zealand and Flanders. Students from Scotland, prior to the establishment of universities in Scotland during the fifteenth and sixteenth centuries, had either to study in England or on the continent. Later Scots students were attracted by courses in law and medicine offered by the Dutch universities. Scottish merchants and craftsmen could be found in towns and cities throughout the Netherlands, especially in Veere, Middelburg, Amsterdam and Rotterdam. Antwerp and later Rotterdam were the great emporiums of northern Europe where colonial products from America, Africa and Asia were distributed. During the seventeenth century Scots communities, with their own churches, could be found throughout Holland and Zealand in particular, and by 1700 around one thousand Scots lived in Rotterdam alone. Some of the Scots found in the Netherlands were religious or political refugees, such as the Covenanters who fled persecution under the Stuart kings to live among their Calvinist brethren. A small number of Dutch merchants and craftsmen also settled in Scotland during the period, some of whom had been attracted in 1672 by the Scots government inviting inhabitants of the United Provinces to come across with the incentive of full naturalization. The Scots were keen to acquire the advanced technological, mercantile and maritime skills of the Dutch.

However, possibly the greatest part of the Scots found in the Netherlands were soldiers fighting in the service of the United Provinces against the Spanish Hapsburgs. The Netherlands were once under the overlordship of the Hapsburg Empire, but the Protestant Reformation of the sixteenth century led to the northern provinces breaking away. For eighty years the Dutch fought to maintain their independence and aiding them in their struggle with Spain were thousands of Scottish soldiers who formed the Scots Brigade. By the end of the eighteenth century the threat generally came from France, during which time the Brigade was generally stationed in Flanders, in what is now Belgium. The Scots Brigade in Dutch Service was founded in 1572 and continued in existence until 1782, during which time a significant number of men from Scotland fought and later settled in the Netherlands. A number of them and their descendants emigrated to the Dutch settlements in America, stretching from the Hudson River to the West Indies and Surinam.

This book, the third volume, identifies some of the Scots who settled in the Netherlands and the Dutch colonies in America between 1575 and 1825 and is based on primary and secondary sources on both sides of the Atlantic. Volume III contains a significant number of marriages that occurred in Rotterdam between Scottish immigrants, and often with local residents. Most occurred in the Scots Kirk or church there but others were held in other Protestant churches. There are also entries based on seventeenth Dutch wills or deeds of Scots, some of whom were bound for the Dutch colonies. Another source was the Court Book of the Scottish Staple at Veere, which identified Scots resident or trading there.

David Dobson

Dundee, Scotland. 2016

ABERCROMBY, G., in Brussels, a letter, 1792.
[NRAS.3955.20.1.83]

ABERCROMBIE, JAMES, from Dundee, married Janet Steedman, from Bo'ness, West Lothian, in the Scots Church in Rotterdam, on 25 April 1744. [GAR]; was admitted as a citizen of Rotterdam in 1753. [GAR]

ABERNETHY, ROBERT, from Scotland, married Annetie Brouwer, from Keulen, [Koln, Germany?], in the Scots Kirk in Rotterdam on 29 October 1673. [GAR]

ADAM, ALEXANDER, from Culross, Fife, married Mary Ferrier, from Rotterdam, in the Scots Kirk in Rotterdam on 14 March 1708. [GAR]

ADAM, ANDREW, from Culross, Fife, son of Alexander Adam, married Margaret Morton, in the Scots Kirk in Rotterdam on 8 August 1726. [GAR]

ADAMS, JAMES, from Bo'ness, West Lothian, married Elizabeth Thomson, from Bo'ness, in the Scots Kirk in Rotterdam on 30 September 1708. [GAR]

ADAM, GEORGE, graduated from Leiden University, Holland, in 1703. [UL]

ADAM, ROBERT, in Brussels, a letter, 1754; in Antwerpen and Bergen-op-Zoom, letters, 1757; in Breda, Brabant, a letter, 1760. [NRS.GD18.4748; 4845; 4857]

ADAMSON, JAMES, from Edinburgh, a soldier bound for the West Indies aboard the ship <u>Gent,</u> testament, 20 December 1640, refers to Mathew Paton and his wife Margaret Peters living on the New Hooft. [GAR.ONA.301.78.166]

ADAMSON, JOHN, a young man from Edinburgh, a seaman under Captain Bastiaen, testament, 23 February 1634, refers to his father Adam Anderson and his step-mother Margaret Beveridge living on the Schiedamsdyke, Rotterdam. [GAR.ONA.194.114.182]

ADAMSON, THOMAS, from 'Durckenoij' in Scotland, and his wife Catalina Jansdochter, testament, 19 March 1652. [GAR.ONA.339.194.415]

ADISON, JOHN, graduated from Leiden University, Holland, in 1595. [UL]

AGNEW, ROBERT, in Utrecht, son of John Agnew in Scotland, a letter, 1775. [NRS.GD11391.4.1]

AICKEN, JOHN, from Perth, married Tanneken Jans from Flanders, in Rotterdam on 21 October 1601. [GAR]

AIKEN, ROBERT, from Edinburgh, married Marietje Calis from Rotterdam, in Rotterdam on 14 July 1740. [GAR]

AIKEN, WILLIAM, a servant, was granted a pass to travel from England to Holland on 5 April 1706. [TNA.SP44.390.415a]

AIKMAN, JOHN, from Stirlingshire, married Janet Paterson, in the Scots Kirk in Rotterdam on 9 January 1704. [GAR]

ALEXANDER, ANDREW, a young Scotsman, a seaman under Captain Jan van Nes, testament, 26 August 1641, refers to Elisabeth Duncan widow of John Smith, mother of John Smith the young Scots seaman, living on the Schiedam dyke in Rotterdam. [GAR.ONA.202.224.285]

ALEXANDER, GEORGE, from Aberdeen, was admitted as a citizen of Rotterdam in 1776. [GAR]

ALEXANDER, JAMES a Scot, was married in Bergen-op-Zoom, Brabant, on 18 October 1680. [WBA]

ALLAN, ANDREW, from Dysart, Fife, married Margaret Matthew, from Rotterdam, in the Scots Kirk in Rotterdam on 7 December 1747. [GAR]; was admitted as a citizen of Rotterdam in 1747. [GAR]

ALLAN, JAMES, from Dysart, Fife, was admitted as a citizen of Rotterdam in 1777. [GAR]

ALLAN, JOHN, from Perth, married Janet More, widow of Nicolas Trotter, in Rotterdam on 8 September 1596. [GAR]

ALLAN, JOHN, from Forres, Moray, married Helena Blankert, from Rotterdam, in the Scots Kirk in Rotterdam on 17 May 1738. [GAR]

ALLAN, ROBERT, an elder of the Scots Church in Rotterdam, 1665-1677. [GAR]

ALLAN, ROBERT, a merchant in Rotterdam, was granted the lands of Muiriehall on 14 September 1703. [RGSS.79.257]

ALLARDICE, JOHN, a sailor from Dysart, Fife, before the Scots Court in Veere, Zealand, in 1735. [NRS.RH11.2.1]

ALVES, JOHN, graduated from Leiden University, Holland, in 1714. [UL]

ANDERSON, ALEXANDER, an MD and a surgeon in Veere, Zealand, took an Oath of Allegiance to King George II, in Veere, in 1728; an assessor of the Scots Court at Veere, 1728. In 1738 he was appointed as an executor of the will of Reverend Charles Jervay minister of the Scots Kirk in Rotterdam. [NRS.RH11.2.1]

ANDERSON, GEORGE, was granted a pass to travel from England to Holland on 28 February 1706. [TNA.SP44.390.390]

ANDERSON, JAMES, from Leith, Midlothian, a seaman under Captain Jan Jorisz Munninck, testament, 8 July 1632, refers to Janet Davidson his landlady. [GAR.ONA.192.189.254]

ANDERSON, JAMES, was granted a pass to travel from England to Holland on 19 April 1706. [TNA.SP44.390.434]

ANDERSON, JAMES, ["Jacobus Andrieszoon"], from Scotland, was admitted as a citizen of Rotterdam in 1746. [GAR]

ANDERSON, JOHANNA, from Scotland, was admitted as a citizen of Rotterdam in 1783. [GAR]

ANDERSON, JOHN, a Scottish merchant, was admitted as a burger of Antwerpen, Flanders, in 1539. [SAA]

ANDERSON, JOHN, from Leith, Midlothian, married Annitgen Adriaens, from Gouda, Holland, in Rotterdam on 25 August 1576. [GAR]

ANDERSON, JOHN, graduated from Leiden University, Holland, in 1669. [UL]

ANDERSON, LYSBETH, wife of John Lindsay a Scotsman, living in Captain Ymants's lane, Rotterdam., a testament, 5 December 1619. [GAR.ONA.101/87/119]

ANDERSON, ROBERT, a factor in Veere, Zealand,1680. [NRS.AC7.5]

ANDERSON, THOMAS, from Perth, was admitted as a citizen of Rotterdam in 1769. [GAR]

ANDERSON, WILLIAM, graduated from Leiden University, Holland, in 1720. [UL]

ANDREWS, ALEXANDER, a merchant in Rotterdam, 1744. [NRS.RS42.XIV.458]

ANDREWS, CHRISTINA, wife of Jan Reyncum servant of Captain Boer Jacob, testament, 30 April 1624, refers to her brother John Starres in Scotland and his daughter Janet. [GAR.ONA.53/380/757]

ANDREWS, JAMES, a Scot, was married in Bergen op Zoom, Brabant, on 2 October 1715. [WBA]

'ARIENSZOON, PIETER', a Scotsman, aged 26, a seaman under Vice Admiral Witte Corneliszoon de With, testament, 26 July 1640, refers to a Scottish sweetheart Lijsbet Jansdochter, and James Robertson a Scot. [GAR.ONA.200.248.362]

ARMOR, WILLIAM, graduated from Leiden University, Holland, in 1636. [UL]

ARMSTRONG, FRANCIS, was granted a pass to travel from England to Holland on 5 April 1706. [TNA.SP44.390.415a]

ARNOT, THOMAS, from Aberdeen, was admitted as a citizen of Rotterdam in 1746. [GAR]

ATSON, [?], WALTER, from Edinburgh, was admitted as a citizen of Rotterdam in 1770. [GAR]

AUCHENCLOSS, ROBERT, a Scot, was married in Bergen-op-Zoom, Brabant, on 30 September 1685. [WBA]

AUCHMUTIE, JAMES, from Scotland, married Christian Inch, from Scotland, in the Scots Kirk in Rotterdam on 26 August 1653. [GAR]

AUCHMOUTIE, JOHN, was granted a pass to travel from England to Holland on 31 August 1706. [TNA.SP44.393.49]

AUCHMUTIE, THOMAS, from Scotland, married Helen Dickson, from Scotland, in the Scots Kirk in Rotterdam on 4 July 1645. [GAR]

AUCHTERLONIE, JAMES, from Arbroath, Angus, married Agnes Ramsay, in the Scots Kirk in Rotterdam on 10 February 1701. [GAR]

AUSTIN, ROBERT, a Scot, was married in Bergen op Zoom, Brabant, on 22 January 1695. [WBA]

BAILLIE, JAMES, graduated from Leiden University, Holland, in 1695. [UL]

BAILLIE, JAMES, from Aberdeen, was admitted as a citizen of Rotterdam in 1735. [GAR]

BAILLIE, JOHN, graduated from Leiden University, Holland, in 1699. [UL]

BAILLIE, WILLIAM, of Hardington, a Captain of Buchan's Regiment in Flanders, and Anna, daughter of James Johnston of Schens, a marriage contract of 1697. [NRS.RH9.7.192]

BAILLIE, WILLIAM, a Scot, was married in Bergen op Zoom, Brabant, on 12 January 1702. [WBA]

BAIRD, ALEXANDER, and **JOHN BAIRD,** in Leiden, Holland, letters, 1678. [NRS.RH15.106.281]

BAIRD, ANDREW, graduated from Leiden University, Holland, in 1722. [UL]

BAIRD, ROBERT, in Surinam, letters to Andrew Russell, a Scots merchant in Rotterdam, 1689-1690. [NRS.RH1.2.772-3/773]

BALFOUR, B., in Breda, Brabant, letters, 1683. [NRS.GD406.1.9001/3]

BALFOUR, WILLIAM, a Scottish gunner under Captain Jasper Lieffhebber, testament, 8 May 1626, refers to Hilletgen Trommels wife of James Pratt a Scotsman. [GAR.ONA.106.4.5]

BALLENTINE, ROBERT, from the island of Bute, was admitted as a citizen of Rotterdam in 1728. [GAR]

BALLIOL, JAMES, graduated from Leiden University, Holland, in 1647. [UL]

BALMAIN, DAVID, from Forteviot, Perthshire, married Robina Stoby, from Hamilton, Lanarkshire, in the Scots Kirk in Rotterdam on 5 December 1708. [GAR]

BARCLAY, DAVID, graduated from Leiden University, Holland, in 1582. [UL]

BARCLAY, GEORGE, graduated from Leiden University, Holland, in 1722. [UL]

BARIELL, BARTHOLOMEW, a merchant in Amsterdam, 1714. [NRS.AC9.530]

BARNETT, [Barentss], JOHN, from Caithness, a gunner under Captain Dirck Vijgh, testament, 11 February 1658, refers to James Johnson, a cobbler, and his wife Nelly Davidsdochter living in the Sprincenhof near the Admiralty College in Rotterdam. [GAR.ONA.217.2.05]

BART, ALEXANDER, from Bo'ness, West Lothian, married Greta Gib, from Aberdeen, in the Scots Kirk in Rotterdam on 9 March 1723. [GAR]

BARTLEY, JOHN, from Glasgow, married Marika Van Dalen, from Rotterdam, in the Scots Kirk in Rotterdam on 20 January 1728. [GAR]

BARTON, RICHARD, husband of Margaret daughter of Manasses van Kroller a book-binder, was admitted as a burgess of Edinburgh, on 17 September 1623. [EBR]

BASKEN, ALEXANDER, graduated from Leiden University, Holland, in 1686. [UL]

BATHGATE, JOHN, from 'Quinsehanne', [Kinghorn, Fife?], was admitted as a citizen of Rotterdam on 18 March 1719. [GAR]

BAUTIE, ALEXANDER, factor in Veere, Zealand, 1635. [SHS.6/3]

· **BAUTIE, ROBERT,** collector at Veere, Zealand, 1632. [SHS.6/3]

BAVERTS, MARGERY, a Scottish wife of John Innes a Scot, testament, 19 June 1628. [GAR.ONA.107.16.19]

BAXTER, FRANCIS, a Scot, was married in Bergen op Zoom, Brabant, on 26 January 1650. [WBA]

BAYNE, GEORGE, master of the Swallow of Rotterdam trading between Aberdeen and Zurick Zee, Holland, and Rotterdam in 1746-1747. [NRS.E504.1.2]

BEAN, CONRAD, a Scotsman, a soldier in the company of Colonel Brock, and his wife Aelken Wilbortsdochter, testament, 13 May 1631. [GAR.ONA.108.157.275]

BEAN, DANIEL, from Inverness, was admitted as a citizen of Rotterdam in 1722. [GAR]

BEATT, WILLIAM, a skipper of Kirkcaldy, Fife, to convey William Anderson a skipper of Anstruther, Fife, also Maurice Gourlay and Alexander Brodie, shipwrecked mariners, back to Great Britain, by order of the Scots Court in Veere, Zealand, in 1735. [NRS.RH11.2.1]

BEGG, ALEXANDER, a Scot, was married in Bergen-op-Zoom, Brabant, on 29 July 1733. [WBA]

BEGG, JOHN, from Galloway, was admitted as a citizen of Rotterdam in 1720. [GAR],formerly a vintner in Rotterdam, was appointed master of the Congiery House in Veere, Zealand, in 1728. He died in October 1728. [NRS.RH11.2.1]

BEIR, JOHN, an elder of the Scots Church in Rotterdam, 1684-1687. [GAR]

BELL, ANDREW, son of James Bell in Bo'ness, West Lothian, married Elisabeth Crawford, in the Scots Kirk in Rotterdam on 14 October 1744. [GAR]

BELL, GEORGE, aboard the Black Knight under master Claes Corneliszoon 't Meickmeisje bound for the West Indies, a testament, 24 January 1628, refers to William Johnston a Scotsman. [GAR.NA.128.183.496]

BELL, JOHN, from Bo'ness, West Lothian, married Agnes Adam, from Amsterdam, in the Scots Kirk in Rotterdam on 26 June 1745. [GAR]

BELL, PATRICK, a merchant burgess of Glasgow, and Agare Rennertis of Staverne in Friesland, a contract, 1619. [NRS.RH1.2.443]

BELL, WILLIAM, from Dumfries, married Christina Van Der Velden, from Rotterdam, in the Scots Kirk in Rotterdam on 8 November 1705. [GAR]

BELL, WILLIAM, in Port Glasgow, master of the Jessie trading with St Eustatius and St Martins, Dutch West Indies, in 1777-1780, accounts book. [NRS.CS96.3829]

BERNE, DAVID, from Aberdeen was admitted as a citizen of Rotterdam on 11 July 1709. [GAR]

BETHUNE, ALEXANDER, graduated from Leiden University, Holland, in 1668. [UL]

BETHUNE, JAMES, graduated from Leiden University, Holland, in 1697. [UL]

BETHUNE, JOHN, born in Alness, Easter Ross, on 2 October 1774, second son of Reverend John Bethune and his wife Catherine Munro, in Dornoch, Easter Ross, died in Berbice on 18 April 1819. [SM.66.885][F.7.27]

BETON, DEREK, and his wife Janet Cuthbert, Scots, janitors {?] living on the Roobridge, Rotterdam, testament, 8 January 1635. [GAR.ONA.195.41.76]

BETON, JAMES, graduated from Leiden University, Holland, in 1627. [UL]

BEVERIDGE, HENDRY, from Aberdeen, married Esther Scott, from Stamfordhall, in the Scots Kirk in Rotterdam on 23 June 1782. [GAR]

BIRSE, ["BAIRS"], graduated from Leiden University, Holland, in 1646. [UL]

BISSET, ALEXANDER, an elder of the Scots Church in Rotterdam, 1664. [GAR]

BISSET, JOHN, a merchant in Perth, trading with T. Van Egmont and Sons in Rotterdam, after 1762. [NRS.B59.37,2.2]

BLACK, DANIEL, from the Shetland Islands, married Margaret Todd, from Rotterdam, in the Scots Kirk in Rotterdam on 13 February 1727. [GAR]

BLACK, GEORGE, a merchant from Aberdeen, an assessor of the Scots Court in Veere, Zealand, 1728 1729. [NRS.RH1.2.1]

BLACK, GILBERT, a merchant in Rotterdam, 1707. [NRS.GD30.2214]

BLACK, JOHN, alias Jan Swart, a merchant in Vlissingen, Zealand, grandson and nearest heir to the deceased John Black late Baillie in Dysart, Fife, a sasine, 1789. [Dysart Burgh Sasines]; John Black alias Jan Swart, a merchant in Vlissingen, Zealand, a deed, 7.2.1791. [NRS.B21.5.271]

BLACKATER, GEORGE, a soldier from Scotland, married Elizabeth Ogleby, from Scotland, in the Scots Kirk in Rotterdam on 22 January 1623. [GAR]

BLACKADDER, JAMES, from Edinburgh, was admitted as a citizen of Rotterdam in 1776. [GAR]

BLACKHALL, ROBERT, a Scottish merchant, was admitted as a burger of Antwerpen, Flanders, in 1544. [SAA]

BLACKWOOD, JAMES, son of John Blackwood in Alloa, Clackmannanshire, married Margaret Sim, in the Scots Kirk in Rotterdam on 11 September 1726. [GAR]

BLAIR, JOHN, from Scotland, a soldier under Captain Liefhebber, married Elizabeth Jacobs, from Scotland, in Rotterdam on 18 October 1598. [GAR]

BLAW, THOMAS, son of James Blaw in Culross, Fife, married Margaret Morton, daughter of John Morton in North Berwick, East Lothian, in the Scots Kirk in Rotterdam on 3 January 1714. [GAR]

BLAIR, JOHN, graduated from Leiden University, Holland, in 1696. [UL]

BLAIR, JOHN, graduated from Leiden University, Holland, in 1723. [UL]

BLAIR, JOHN, born 26 February 1741 in Brechin, Angus, son of Reverend David Blair and his wife Christian Doig, settled in Providence, Essequibo. [F.5.376]

BLAIR, LAMBERT, a planter in Demerara during 1790s.

BLAIR, PATRICK, graduated from Leiden University, Holland, in 1737. [UL]

BLAIR, ROBERT, graduated from Leiden University, Holland, in 1675. [UL]

BLAIR, THOMAS, graduated from Leiden University, Holland, in 1792. [UL]

BLOCK, JOHN, a Dutch sea-captain, was admitted as a burgess of Edinburgh, on 11 December 1649. [EBR]

BOATH, CHRISTOPHER, burgess of Veere, Zealand, a deed, 17 March 1560. [NRS.RDIV.90]

BOGIE, JAMES, born 1623 in Edinburgh, a corporal, later sergeant, in the service of the Dutch West India Company, bound aboard the Stockfish for Brazil, 1641, married Elizabeth Trail in Tobago, served in Angola, a deed 1656. [GAA.NA.1281/167; 1291/161;1306/214]

BOGLE, GEORGE, graduated from Leiden University, Holland, in 1731. [UL]

BORLAND, JOHN, a Scottish merchant in Boston, New England, shipped a cargo of furs aboard the Dolphin of Boston, master Michael 'Schuill'?, bound for Amsterdam and Andrew Russell a Scots merchant there, 7 September 1693. [NRS.GD1.885.2]

BORUTE, DAVID, a solicitor in Middelburg, Zealand, a deed, 1702. [NRS.RD2.86.2.163]

BOSWELL, DAVID, formerly a Captain of Colonel Edward Preston's Regiment in Flanders, 1693. [NRS.GD226.18.8]

BOSWELL, JAMES, graduated from Leiden University, Holland, in 1695. [UL]

BOSWELL, JOHN, an MD graduate of the University of Leiden, Holland, a certificate of disjunction from the Royal College of Physicians of Edinburgh in 1748. [NRAS.726.3.63]

BOTHWELL, FRANCIS, graduated from Leiden University, Holland, in 1589. [UL]

BOUXEN, HUYBRECHT, a merchant in Holland, 1736. [NRS.AC9.1355]

BOW, JOHN, from Airth, Stirlingshire, married Christian Young, daughter of James Young in Queensferry, West Lothian, in the Scots Kirk in Rotterdam on22 September 1701. [GAR]

BOWIE, JOHN, was granted a pass to travel from England to Holland on 24 December 1705. [TNA.SP44.390.355]

BOWIE, PHILIP MACDONALD, took the Oath of Association in Den Haag, 1696. [TNA]

BOWMAN, GEORGE, a Scot from Aberdeen, serving under Captain Andries Soutendael, testament, 20 October 1627, refers to Alexander Mackenzie, a Scot, and his wife Annetgen Dircksdochter. [GAR.ONA.106.192.264]

BOYD, CHARLES, a Captain of General Collier's Regiment, and his wife Katherine Van Beest, a bond for 6000 marks, dated 20 July 1714. [NRS.GD3.975]

BOYLE, AGNES, widow of John Key, a tailor in St Eustatia, Dutch West Indies, 1782. [NRS.CS17.1.1/28]

BOYLE, DAVID, from Darnichen, [Dunnichen, Angus?], married Isobel Eaton from Brechin, Angus, in the Scots Kirk in Rotterdam on 30 August 1741. [GAR]; from Montrose, Angus, was admitted as a citizen of Rotterdam in 1747. [GAR]

BRAID, JOHN, ['**Jonij Bredde**'], a Scottish baker in Veere, Zealand, an inventory, 1537. [GAV.Inv.920]

BREBNER SINCLAIR and Company, merchants in Glasgow, trading with Surinam and St Eustatius, 1778-1782.. [NRS.CS96.1413.14]

BREMER, JAMES, from Aberdeen, married Elizabeth Key, from Bo'ness, West Lothian, in the Scots Kirk in Rotterdam on 11 March 1705. [GAR]

BRESTON, JAMES, graduated from Leiden University, Holland, in 1698. [UL]

BRIDGES, WILLIAM, from Leven in Fife, married Christian White daughter of Allan White in Rotterdam, in the Scots Kirk in Rotterdam on 18 November 1705. [GAR]

BRISBANE, GEORGE, from Glasgow, married Margaret Wallace, from Rotterdam, in the Scots Kirk in Rotterdam on 29 April 1735. [GAR]

BRORK, WILLEM, a Dutch harpooner aboard the City of Aberdeen of Aberdeen whaling off Greenland in 1754. [NRS.E508.51.8]

BROUN, ADRIAAN ANTONY, born 1732 in Veere, Zealand, a merchant and planter in Zealand and the West Indies, a member of the Scots Court in Veere and also of the Scots church there, he died in 1784. [ZA]

BROWN, ADAM, from Edinburgh, a seaman, testament, 16 December 1649, refers to David Jans and his wife Neeltge Jans living in Dortmans Alley on the Schiedam dyke, Rotterdam, Captain Jacob Peis of Middelburg, Zealand, Captain Abram Dominicuszoon, and Captain Droochbroot. [GAR.ONA.210.163.332]

BROWN, DAVID, from Leith, Midlothian, widower of Elisabeth Boys, a quartermaster under Captain Jan Jansz. Van der Linde, testament refers to cousin William Dickson from Leith, 1 July 1616. [GAR.ONA.28/52/100]

BROWN, DAVID, a Scot, was married in Bergen op Zoom Brabant, on 6 September 1719. [WBA]

BROWN, JOHN, from Ferriton, husband of Jane Houston, in Amsterdam, 1640, brother-in-law of James Houston a merchant in Amsterdam and son-in-law of John Houston a merchant in Edinburgh. [GAA.NA.849/9]

BROWNE, J., in Antwerpen, Flanders, 1739. [NRS.GD24.3.389]

BROWN, ROBERT, minister of the Scots Kirk in Veere, Zealand, ca.1653. [SSV.300]

BROWN, THOMAS, Scotsman, and his wife Catherine Henderson, testament, 16 June 1636. [GAR.ONA.196.116.218]

BROWN, THOMAS, from Leith, Midlothian, a seaman under Captain Joost van Coulster, bound for Brasil, testament, 8

December 1647, refers to James Gordon and his wife Mary Ford. [GAR.ONA.209.62.112]

BROWN, THOMAS, son of Alexander Brown a carrier in Glasgow, an apprentice hammerman in Glasgow, absconded and enlisted in Drumlanrig's regiment bound for Holland, 1748. [NRS.AC10.341]

BROWN, WILLIAM, from Edinburgh, married Josyntje Jacobs, from Rotterdam, in Rotterdam on 11 August 1715. [GAR]

BROWN, WILLIAM, from Wemyss, Fife, was admitted as a citizen of Rotterdam on 23 August 1719. [GAR]

BRUCE, ANDREW, was granted a pass to travel from England to Holland on 20 May 1706. [TNA.SP44.390.455]

BRUCE, Lord CHARLES BRUDENAL, graduated from Leiden University, Holland, in 1789. [UL]

BRUCE, JOHN, in Brussels and Antwerpen, Flanders, a letter, 1683. [NRS.GD29.2192]

BRUCE, ROBERT, in Rotterdam, letters, 1675. [NRS.GD331.48]

BRUCE, ROBERT, from Stirling, married Judith Willems from Rotterdam, in the Scots Kirk in Rotterdam on 3 October 1717. [GAR]

BRYCE, JOHN, a young man, a seaman under Captain Corstiaen Elderszoon, bound for Denmark, testament, 8 May 1659, refers to Richard Falconer and his wife Margaret Anderson, living in Jan Slijpen Alley on the Schiedam dyke, also to John Mitchell a smith in Airth, Stirlingshire. [GAR.ONA.217.90.321]

BRYSON, ABRAHAM, from Lyle in West Flanders, was admitted as a burgess of Edinburgh on 23 July 1633. [EBR]

BUCHAN, ROBERT, from Elphinstone, East Lothian, was admitted as a citizen of Rotterdam on 23 September 1720. [GAR]

BUCHAN, ["BOUCHAM"], THOMAS, graduated from Leiden University, Holland, in 1700. [UL]

BUCHANAN, DAVID, in Amsterdam, 1640. [GAA.NA.956/3/52]

BUCHANAN, JAMES, from Montrose, Angus, was admitted as a citizen of Rotterdam in 1778. [GAR]

BUCHANAN, JOHN, from Banff, married Elizabeth McNeil, daughter of Neil McNeil, in the Scots Kirk in Rotterdam on 18 August 1763. [GAR]

BUCHANAN and SIMPSON, merchants in Glasgow, importing tobacco from Virginia and Maryland, exporting tobacco to Rotterdam, journals, 1758-1761. [NRS.CS96.504]

BURNET, ALEXANDER, graduated from Leiden University, Holland, in 1696. [UL]

BURNET, JOHN, factor and collector at Veere, Zealand, 1631. [SHS.6/3]

BURNETT, JOHN, graduated from Leiden University, Holland, in 1675. [UL]

BURNETT, JOHN, from Aberdeen, was admitted as a citizen of Rotterdam in 1756. [GAR]

BURNETT, THOMAS, possibly the Thomas Burnett a factor in Dort [Dordrecht], Holland, and a burgess of Dundee, 1669, [DBR]; a merchant in Rotterdam, 1675. [GAA.NA.3864/133]

BURNETT, THOMAS, graduated from Leiden University, Holland, in 1688. [UL]

BURNIE, JEAN, from Aberdeen, was admitted as a citizen of Rotterdam on 12 September 1716. [GAR]

BURT, ROBERT, an elder of the Scots Church in Rotterdam, 1658-1660. [GAR]

CADMAN, WILLIAM, from Edinburgh, married Maertgen Stoffels, in Rotterdam on 17 August 1608. [GAR]

CALDOM, ROBERT, an elder of the Scots Church in Rotterdam, 1667-1680. [GAR]

CALDWELL, ANNE, was granted a pass to travel from England to Holland on 21 September 1706. [TNA.SP44.393.95]

CALDWELL, ROBERT, was granted a pass to travel from England to Holland on 19 November 1705. [TNA.SP44.390.335]

CALENDAR, JOHN, from Stirling, married Mary Obyn, in the Scots Kirk in Rotterdam on 24 January 1701. [GAR]

CALENDAR, JOHN, from Leith, Midlothian, and Christina Bruydt from Rotterdam, were married in Rotterdam on 17 August 1704. [GAR]

CALENDAR, WALTER, and Euphan Burnside, both from Bo'ness, West Lothian, were married in the Scots Kirk in Rotterdam on 2 May 1714. [GAR]

CAMERON, ANGUS, from Argyll , was admitted as a citizen of Rotterdam in 1754. [GAR];married Helen Ross a widow, in the Scots Kirk in Rotterdam on 22 September 1753. [GAR]

CAMERON, JAMES, from Scotland, was admitted as a citizen of Rotterdam in 1768. [GAR]

CAMERON, JOHN, a merchant in Berbice, 1817, 1820. [NRS.RD5.124.257; RD5.191.483]

CAMPBELL, ALEXANDER, from Glasgow, a seaman under Captain Maerten Harperszoon Tromp, testament, 2 July 1629, refers to Janet Brown, widow of Andrew Sampson, Thomas Bacon an Englishman, and Robert Burt a Scots clothmaker. [GAR.ONA.189.158.259]

CAMPBELL, ALEXANDER, graduated from Leiden University, Holland, in 1680. [UL]

CAMPBELL, ARCHIBALD, graduated from Leiden University, Holland, in 1720. [UL]

CAMPBELL, ARCHIBALD, in Surinam, documents, 1802. [NRS.RH4.196.3]

CAMPBELL, CHARLES, from Edinburgh, married Elizabeth Wilson from London, in the Scots Kirk in Rotterdam on 11 April 1715. [GAR]

CAMPBELL, CHARLES, graduated from Leiden University, Holland, in 1738. [UL]

CAMPBELL, COLIN, of Ardmaddy, Argyll. in Utrecht, a letter, 1700. [NRS.GD112.39.161.13]

CAMPBELL, COLIN, graduated from Leiden University, Holland, in 1727. [UL]

CAMPBELL, COLIN, graduated from Leiden University, Holland, in 1740. [UL]

CAMPBELL, COLIN, of the Good Success plantation, Essequibo, died in Georgetown, Demerara, on 29 September 1822. [SM.91.128]

CAMPBELL, DAVID, from Glasgow, was admitted as a citizen of Rotterdam on 6 January 1711. [GAR]

CAMPBELL, DOUGALL, a Scot, was married in Bergen op Zoom, Brabant, on 21 June 1719. [WBA]

CAMPBELL, EDWARD, from Kilmichael, married Janet Robertson, from Stirling, in the Scots Kirk in Rotterdam on 30 March 1730. [GAR]

CAMPBELL, GEORGE, a poor man, was granted a pass to travel from England to Holland on 10 October 1705. [TNA.SP44.391.172]

CAMPBELL, HENRY, graduated from Leiden University, Holland, in 1740. [UL]

CAMPBELL, JAMES, from Bo'ness, West Lothian, was admitted as a citizen of Rotterdam on 5 April 1719. [GAR]

CAMPBELL, JOHN, graduated from Leiden University, Holland, in 1700. [UL]

CAMPBELL, JOHN, graduated from Leiden University, Holland, in 1716. [UL]

CAMPBELL, JOHN, graduated from Leiden University, Holland, in 1740. [UL]

CAMPBELL, JOHN, son of Patrick Campbell of the Royal Bank of Scotland in Edinburgh, died in Berbice on 10 December 1805. [SM.68.78][EEC.1806]

CAMPBELL, PATRICK, graduated from Leiden University, Holland, in 1702. [UL]

CAMPBELL, PATRICK, graduated from Leiden University, Holland, in 1726. [UL]

CAMPBELL, PATRICK, graduated from Leiden University, Holland, in 1739. [UL]

CAMPBELL, ROBERT, graduated from Leiden University, Holland, in 1719. [UL]

CAMPBELL, ROBERT, graduated from Leiden University, Holland, in 1739. [UL]

CAMPBELL, THOMAS, in Grenada, died in Demerara during 1795. [SM.57.359]

CAMPBELL, WILLIAM, graduated from Leiden University, Holland, in 1727. [UL]

CAMPBELL, WILLIAM, frm Montrose, Angus, was admitted as a citizen of Rotterdam in 1746. [GAR]

CANT, ELIZABETH, mistress of the Conciergery House in Veere, Zealand, widow of ......Porterfield, mother of John and Walter Porterfield, died in July 1643. [SSV.294]

CANTLEY, JAMES, from Aberdeen, was admitted as a citizen of Rotterdam in 1775. [GAR]

CARLISLE, ALEXANDER, graduated from Leiden University, Holland, in 1745. [UL]

CARLYLE, CATHERINE, from Annandale, Dumfries-shire, was admitted as a citizen of Rotterdam on 25 May 1717. [GAR]

CARMICHAEL, ANNE, and her child, was granted a pass to travel from England to Holland on 14 September 1706. [TNA.SP44.393.87]

CARMICHAEL, DOUGAL, from Edinburgh, married Mary Grindlay, from Leith, Midlothian, in the Scots Kirk in Rotterdam on 21 January 1756. [GAR]

CARMICHAEL, GERSHOM, graduated from Leiden University, Holland, in 1739. [UL]

CARMICHAEL, JAMES, graduated from Leiden University, Holland, in 1639. [UL]

CARMICHAEL, JAMES, graduated from Leiden University, Holland, in 1735. [UL]

CARMICHAEL, JOHN, graduated from Leiden University, Holland, in 1721. [UL]

CARMICHAEL, JOHN, graduated from Leiden University, Holland, in 1735. [UL]

CARMICHAEL, THOMAS, graduated from Leiden University, Holland, in 1723. [UL]

CARNEGIE, JOHN, graduated from Leiden University, Holland, in 1700. [UL]

CARNEGIE, KENTIGERN, graduated from Leiden University, Holland, in 1686. [UL]

CARNEGIE, ROBERT, graduated from Leiden University, Holland, in 1710. [UL]

CARR, JOHN, from Edinburgh, married Lysbet Diericks, from Rotterdam, in Rotterdam on 12 December 1593. [GAR]

CARR, JOHN, from Linlithgow, West Lothian, a seaman aboard the Utrecht, Captain du Bois, testament, 26 February 1666, refers to Alexander Nicoll, a seafarer, and Greta Watt his wife. [GAR.ONA.919.211.600]

CARR, MAGNUS, son of Magnus Carr in Stromness, Orkney, married Martha McKenzie, from Rotterdam, in the Scots Kirk in Rotterdam on 18 August 1770. [GAR]

CAR, WILLIAM, graduated from Leiden University, Holland, in 1626. [UL]

CARRUTHERS, THOMAS, graduated from Leiden University, Holland, in 1729. [UL]

CARSE, JOHN, was granted a pass to travel from England to Holland on 21 September 1706. [TNA.SP44.393.91]

CARSTAIRS, ALEXANDER, a merchant in Rotterdam, a letter, 1692; 1732. [NRS.CS96/1726/17; AC9.1185]; 1703. [NRS.AC9.23]; an elder of the Scots Church in Rotterdam, 1698-1722. [GAR]

CARSTAIRS, ALEXANDER, was appointed deputy Conservator of the Scots Privileges in the Netherlands at Veere, Zealand, in 1734. [NRS.RH11.2.1]

CARSTAIRS, WILLIAM, graduated from Leiden University, Holland, in 1686. [UL]; in Den Haag, Holland, a letter, 1687. [NRS.GD158.1031]; in Breda, Brabant, a letter, 1693. [NRS.GDD406.1.3772]

CARSTAIRS, W. A., a Member of the Supreme Court, died in Surinam on 1 November 1821. [EEC.17244][S.261]

CASS, RICHARD, graduated from Leiden University, Holland, in 1647. [UL]

CASSILLS, DAVID, from Bo'ness, West Lothian, was admitted as a citizen of Rotterdam in 1721. [GAR]

CASTELLAW, WILLIAM, graduated from Leiden University, Holland, in 1663. [UL]

CATENACH, THOMAS, from Edinburgh, was admitted as a citizen of Rotterdam in 1754. [GAR]

CATENACH, WILLIAM, a merchant in Rotterdam, 1729. [NRS.CS228.B2.35]

CATHCART, CHARLES, graduated from Leiden University, Holland, in 1737. [UL]

CATHCART, FREDERICK, second son of William, Earl of Cathcart, married Jean MacAdam of Craigengillan, in Berbice on 18 October 1822. [EEC.18113]

CATHCART, JAMES, graduated from Leiden University, Hollaand, in 1657. [UL]

CATHCART, JOHN, graduated from Leiden University, Holland, on 31 August 1737. [UL]

CAVELING, WILLIAM, from Linlithgow, West Lothian, a tailor in Bergen-op-Zoom, inventory, 1507. [GAB.Inv.3092.105r]

CHALMERS, GEORGE, graduated from Leiden University, Holland, on 4 April 1715. [UL]

CHALMERS, JAMES, graduated from Leiden University, Holland, on 5 December 1686. [UL]

CHALMERS, PATRICK, graduated from Leiden University, Holland, on 18 September 1679. [UL]

CHALMERS, ROBERT, graduated from Leiden University, Holland,on 4 May 1688. [UL]

CHALMERS, JOHN, minister of the Scots Kirk in Veere, Zealand, took an Oath of Allegiance to King George II, in Veere, in 1728. [NRS.RH11.2.1]

CHALMERS, ROBERT, a Scots seaman under Captain Sier de Liefde, and his wife Janet Watt living in Raem Street, Rotterdam, testament, 13 May 1651. [GAR.ONA.212.21.36]

CHAPMAN, LEONARD, graduated from Leiden University, Holland, on 15 August 1727. [UL]

CHARLES, WILLIAM, from Edinburgh, a seaman aboard the Maestricht bound for the East Indies, testament, 5 January 1642, refers to his stepmother Anne Jamieson, widow of his father James Charles living in Edinburgh, and William Johnson, a Scotsman, and his wife Elisabeth Williamson, living on the Schiedam dyke. [GAR.ONA.202.329.461]

CHARLES, JOHN, from Edinburgh, a seaman aboard the Maestricht bound for the East Indies, testament, 5 January 1642, refers to his stepmother Anne Jamieson, widow of his father James Charles living in Edinburgh, and William Johnson, a Scotsman, and his wife Elisabeth Williamson, living on the Schiedam dyke. [GAR.ONA.202.329.461]

CHARTERS, LAURENCE, from the Lothians, graduated from Leiden University, Holland, on 22 September 1662. [UL]

CHEAP, JAMES, graduated from Leiden University, Holland, in March 1700. [UL]

CHEISLEY, WALTER, graduated from Leiden University, Holland, on 12 December 1689. [UL]

CHEYNE, ARTHUR, graduated from Leiden University, Holland, on 24 April 1653. [UL]

CHEYNE, FRANCIS, from Aberdeen, a seaman under Admiral Tromp, testament, 24 February 1646, refers to James Frissell and his wife Elizabeth Davidsdochter. [GAR.ONA.207.211.320]

CHISHOLM, ALEXANDER, son of Provost William Chisholm of Inverness, died on Friendship Plantation, Demerara, on 16 July 1799. [GC.1190]

CHISHOLM, DANIEL, from Inverness-shire, married Catherine Wilson, from Hamilton, Lanarkshire, in the Scots Kirk in Rotterdam on 12 October 1769. [GAR]

CHISHOLM, DANIEL, from Inverness-shire, married Hyndrynt van der Glas, from Leiden, Holland, in the Scots Kirk in Rotterdam on 16 January 1771. [GAR]

CHISHOLM, EWAN, from Kilmorack, Inverness-shire, married Elizabeth Black, daughter of John Black in London, in Rotterdam on 8 June 1767. [GAR]; was admitted as a citizen of Rotterdam in 1773. [GAR]

CHISHOLM, HENRY, graduated from Leiden University, Holland, on 6 September 1726. [UL]

CHISHOLM, JAMES, graduated from Leiden University, Holland, on 7 March 1696. [UL]

CHRISTIE, ALEXANDER, from Edinburgh, graduated from Leiden University, Holland, on 1 May 1671. [UL]

CHRISTIE, JOHN, from Leith, Midlothian, married Tauntje Jans, from Amersfoort, in Rotterdam on 3 January 1644. [GAR]

CHRISTIE, JOHN, graduated from Leiden University, Holland, on 31 August 1684. [UL]

CHRISTIE, JOHN, an elder of the Scots Church in Rotterdam, 1679-1706. [GAR]

CLAASEN, HENDRICK, master of the Veede van Grow, trading between Rotterdam and Perth in 1757. [NRS.E504.27.3]

CLAESS, THOMAS, a Scottish shoemaker in Veere, Zealand, inventory, 1547. [GAV.Inv.920]

CLARK, ADAM, a Scot, was married in Bergen-op-Zoom on 11 October 1702. [WBA]

CLERK, DAVID, graduated from Leiden University, Holland, on 15 October 1746 [UL]

CLARK, DUNCAN, from Inverness, was admitted as a citizen of Rotterdam in 1766. [GAR]

CLERK, GEORGE, graduated from Leiden University, Holland, on 12 May 1642. [UL]

CLERK, GEORGE, graduated from Leiden University, Holland, on 13 January 1736. [UL]

CLARK, GEORGE, from Aberdeen, was admitted as a citizen of Rotterdam in 1788. [GAR]

CLERK, JAMES, graduated from Leiden University, Holland, on 14 August 1731. [UL]

CLERK, JAMES, in Leiden, son of Sir John Clerk of Penicuik, Midlothian, a letter, 1738. [NRS.GD18.1067]

CLARK, JAMES, graduated from Leiden University, Holland, on 12 May 1741. [UL]

CLARK, JOHN, graduated from Leiden University, Holland, on 29 September 1695. [UL]

CLARK, JOHN, a merchant in Amsterdam, 1723. [GAA.NA.8599/818]

CLARK, JOHN, graduated from Leiden University, Holland, on 1 November 1737. [UL]

CLERK, ROBERT, graduated from Leiden University, Holland, on 6 January 1727. [UL]

CLERK, ROBERT, from Edinburgh, graduated from Leiden University, Holland, on 7 June 1783. [UL]

CLARK, THOMAS, graduated from Leiden University, Holland, on 26 March 1776. [UL]

CLARK, WILLIAM, a merchant trading with the Low Countries, from Leith to Holland in 1700, visited Veere, Middleburg, Rotterdam, Dort, Delft, Leiden and Amsterdam. [NRS.GD1.1432.5]

CLARK, WILLIAM, graduated from Leiden University, Holland, on 29 September 1734. [UL]

CLARK, WILLIAM, from Inverness, was admitted as a citizen of Rotterdam in 1758. [GAR]

CLELLAND, ROBERT, in Utrecht, a letter, 1692. [NRS.RH9.2.60]

CLELAND, WILLIAM, graduated from Leiden University, Holland, on 4 October 1680. [UL]

CLEPHAN, JAMES, son of William Clephan, graduated from Leiden University, Holland, on 2 November 1724. [UL]

CLEPHAN, JOHN, son of William Clephan, graduated from Leiden University, Holland, on 2 November 1724. [UL]

CLEPHAN, WILLIAM, graduated from Leiden University, Holland, on 2 November 1724. [UL]

CLEPHANE, Dr, in Groningen, 1731, as tutor to Lord Everard Manners. [NRS.GD1.726.1]

CLERY, GEORGE, graduated from Leiden University, Holland, on 27 September 1618. [UL]

CLOUSTOUN, SIMON, master of the Fleand Hart of Inkusen in Holland, at Dundee, 1564. [Dundee Burgh Court Records, 27 November 1564]

CLUNES, JAMES, from the Shetland Islands, married Margaret Manson, from the Shetland Islands, in the Scots Kirk in Rotterdam on 5 March 1744. [GAR]

CLYDESDALE, JAMES, graduated from Leiden University, Holland, on 15 September 1790. [UL]

COCHRAN, ALEXANDER, son of Archibald Cochran in Linlithgow, West Lothian, married Janet Bannit, in the Scots Kirk in Rotterdam on 28 December 1707. [GAR], was admitted as a citizen of Rotterdam in 1727. [GAR]

COCHRAN, CHARLES, graduated from Leiden University, Holland, on 19 September 1724. [UL]

COCHRAN, JAMES, a law student in Utrecht, 1724, son of James Cochran of Waterside, a witness. [NRS.GD84.1.33.1]

COCHRANE, WILLIAM, graduated from Leiden University, Holland, on 22 October 1709. [UL]

COCKBURN, ADAM, from Edinburgh, graduated from Leiden University, Holland, on 24 November 1793. [UL]

COCKBURN, ALEXANDER, graduated from Leiden University, Holland, on 14 November 1687. [UL]

COCKBURN, ARCHIBALD, graduated from Leiden University, Holland, on 28 August 1692. [UL]

COCKBURN, ARCHIBALD, graduated from Leiden University, Holland, on 12 March 1709. [UL]

COCKBURN, BARBARA, aged 16, daughter of James Cockburn living on the Schiedam dyke in the 'Scotch Ship', testament, 5 September 1651, refers to her mother Janet Hamilton. [GAR.ONA.212.79.157]

COCKBURN, JAMES, merchant and master of the Vulcan in Rotterdam, 1644. [GAA.NA.849.50]

COCKBURN, JOHN, graduated from Leiden University, Holland, on 23 April 1675. [UL]

COCKBURN, JOHN, graduated from Leiden University, Holland, on 23 June 1676. [UL]

COCKBURN, PATRICK, graduated from Leiden University, Holland, on 15 July 1699. [UL]

COCKBURN, PATRICK, graduated from Leiden University, Holland, on 2 November 1725. [UL]

COCKBURN, RICHARD, graduated from Leiden University, Holland, on 30 December 1727. [UL]

COCKBURN, ROBERT, graduated from Leiden University, Holland, on 23 August 1720. [UL]

COLLIER, JAMES, graduated from Leiden University, Holland, on 25 May 1782. [UL]

COLME, ARCHIBALD, graduated from Leiden University, Holland, on 13 April 1694. [UL]

COLQUHOUN, ALEXANDER, was granted a pass to travel from England to Holland on 11 May 1706. [TNA.SP44.390.450]

COLQUHOUN, ARCHIBALD, graduated from Leiden University, Holland, on 18 October 1681. [UL]

COLQUHOUN, Sir GEORGE, Captain of Colonel Gordon's Regiment in the service of the United Provinces, a deposition, 1764. [NRS.GD237.19.127]

COLQUHOUN, JOHN, graduated from Leiden University, Holland, on 19 May 1648. [UL]

COLVILL, ROBERT, graduated from Leiden University, Holland, on 7 April 1687. [UL]

COLVIN, JOHN, graduated from Leiden University, Holland, on 13 October 1656. [UL]

COLVIN, ROBERT, from Stirling, a seaman under Commander Dirck Janszoon, testament, 26 April 1653, refers to his sister Janet Colvin on the Schiedam dyke. [GAR.ONA.214.64.191]

COMRIE, ALEXANDER, graduated from Leiden University, Holland, on 10 July 1733. [UL]

COMRIE, ARCHIBALD, graduated from Leiden University, Holland, on 23 November 1706. [UL]

COMRIE, JOHN, graduated from Leiden University, Holland, on 13 December 1670. [UL]

COMYN, PATRICK, graduated from Leiden University, Holland, on 21 February 1684. [UL]

COMMYNS, WILLIAM, from Leith, Midlothian, married Elizabeth Failler, in Rotterdam on 13 November 1735. [GAR]

CONNELL, DAVID, graduated from Leiden University, Holland, on 19 September 1732. [UL]

CONNELL, MATTHEW, graduated from Leiden University, Holland, on 27 May 1701. [UL]

CONNELLY, JEAN, relict of John Petry a soldier, now spouse of George Reynolds, a soldier in Lieutenant General Sinclair's Regiment of Foot, married in Brugge, Flanders, on 8 June 1744. [NRS.CC8.6.340]

COOPER, DAVID, a tutor in Utrecht, a witness, 1724. [NRS.GD84.1.33.1]

CORBET, SAMUEL, from Greenock, Renfrewshire, married Marion Carck, from Geertruiden, in the Scots Kirk in Rotterdam on 12 December 1726. [GAR]

CORNELIUS, BOOIJ, a Dutch harpooner aboard the City of Aberdeen of Aberdeen whaling off Greenland in 1754. [NRS.E508.51.8]

CORNFOOT, ANDREW JAMES, born 1807 in Largo, Fife, died at Burnside, Surinam, in 1830. [BM.28.574]

COURTIER, ANDREW, an elder of the Scots Church in Rotterdam, 1658-1675. [GAR]

COUSINS, WILLIAM, from Scotland, was admitted as a citizen of Rotterdam in 1756. [GAR]

COUSTON, GEORGE, from Edinburgh, husband of Margaret Houston, in Amsterdam, brother-in-law of James Houston a merchant in Amsterdam and son-in-law of John Houston a merchant in Edinburgh. [GAA.NA.849/9]

COUTTS, ['COETSIUS'], ALEXANDER, graduated from Leiden University, Holland, on 22 June 1619. [UL]

COUTTS, JOHN, from Aberdeen, married Helen Taylor, from Rotterdam, in the Scots Kirk in Rotterdam on 29

November 1763. [GAR]; was admitted as a citizen of Rotterdam in 1763. [GAR]

COWAN, THOMAS, from Falkirk, Stirlingshire, married Mary van der Leer, from Schiedam, in the Scots Kirk in Rotterdam on 25 March 1711. [GAR]

COWIE, DAVID, a merchant bound for the East Indies, testament empowers Daniel Johnson, a Scot, to collect his assets to give to his brother Alexander Cowie in Culross, Fife, 19 August 1619. [GAR.ONA.101/42/53]

COWDEN, JAMES, son of Peter Cowden in Edinburgh, bound for the East Indies under Captain Jacob den Boudt, testament, 29 November 1607. [GAR.ONA.25/267/572]

CRAIG, DANIEL, a Scot, was married in Bergen-op-Zoom,Brabant, on 24 December 1758. [WBA]

CRAWFORD ["Kraffort"], DAVID, a mason, with his wife and daughter, from the Netherlands aboard the Fox bound for the New Netherlands, 2 September 1662. [GAR]

CRAWFORD, DAVID, a soldier in Captain James Douglas's Company of Grenadiers in Holland, was court-martialled for mutiny in 1691. [NRS.E99.41.145]

CRAWFORD, DAVID, a merchant in St Eustatia, eldest son of David Crawford a merchant in Dublin, grandson of Andrew Crawford of Crawfordston, a deed, 1773. [NRS.RD4.213.1232]

CRAWFORD, GRANT, in Rotterdam, a letter, 1739. [NRS.GD110.1112]

CRAWFORD, JAMES, from Edinburgh, was admitted as a citizen of Rotterdam in 1736. [GAR]

CRAWFORD, JAMES, was appointed Conservator of the Scots Privileges at Veere, Zealand, in 1782. [SSV.263]

CRAWFORD, PATRICK, in Rotterdam, trading with James Penman in Charleston, South Carolina, in 1768. [NRAS.771.491]; was appointed Conservator of the Scots

Privileges at Veere, Zealand, in 1769. [SSV.260] He died in 1782 and was succeeded by his brother James. {SSV.263}]

CRAWFORD, PETER, from Scotland, was admitted as a citizen of Rotterdam in 1754. [GAR]

CRICHTON, JOHN, in Leiden, Holland, a letter, 1690; in Den Haag, a letter, 1691. [NRS.GD158.69.70/119]

CROW, JOHN, porter on the Delftse Port, testament, 4 July 1650, refers to his wife Elisabeth Sander living on Raems Street, Rotterdam. [GAR.ONA.211.91.171]

CRUICKSHANK, ALEXANDER, eldest son of Dr Cruickshank in Haughs of Corsie, died in Nickerie, Surinam, on 13 September 1820. [SM.86.383]

CRUICKSHANKS, GEORGE, a merchant in Rotterdam, petitioned the Scots Court in Veere, Zealand, in 1719 re his appointment as master of the Congiery House in Veere. [NRS.RH11 2 1]; was admitted as a citizen of Rotterdam on 7 December 1718. [GAR]

CRUIKSHANK, JAMES, from Aberdeen, was admitted as a citizen of Rotterdam in 1740. [GAR]

CRUIKSHANK, PATRICK, from Aberdeen, later in Holland, 1720. [NRS.AC9.671]; was admitted as a citizen of Rotterdam in 1735. [GAR]

CUMMIN, ALEXANDER, was appointed Precentor of the Scots Kirk in Veere, Zealand, in 1648. [SSV.283]

CUMMING, Sir ALEXANDER, was granted a pass to travel from England to Holland on 5 April 1706. [TNA.SP44.390.415a]

CUMING, ALEXANDER, carpenter aboard the Unity of Aberdeen, master John Lumsdale, before the Scots Court in Veere, Zealand, in 1739. [NRS.RH11.2.1]

CUMMING, JAMES, a merchant in Breda, Brabant, spouse Vera Chalmers, a sasine, 2 January 1772, parents of Helen

Cumming spouse of William Brand a merchant in Leith, Midlothian. [NRS.RS27.196.136]

CUMING, LACHLAN, from Morayshire, a planter in the Dutch colony of Demerara by 1791. [Essequibo and Demerary Royal Gazette, 18 April 1812]

CUMING, THOMAS, born 1740 in Dallas, Morayshire, settled a planter in Dutch Demerara during 1760s, married [1] into a Dutch family, [2] Isabella Fraser, a politician there before 1796, founder of Stabroek alias Cumingburg, died in 1815. [Dallas MI, Morayshire]; a marriage contract with Isabella, daughter of Colonel Fraser of Belladrum, Inverness-shire, dated 27 September 1798. [NRS.RD5,31.279]

CUMMINS, THOMAS, from Wemyss, Fife, married Margaret Gray, from Rotterdam, in the Scots Kirk in Rotterdam on 1 December 1700. [GAR]

CUMMING, THOMAS, in Demerara, referred to in the will of Robert Elliot in Demerara, 1779. [NRS.RD4.235.748]

CUMMINGS, WILLIAM, from Leith, Midlothian, was admitted as a citizen of Rotterdam in 1730. [GAR]

CUNNINGHAM, ADAM, a prisoner of the Spanish in Ostende, Flanders, papers, 1677-1678, brother of Sir John Cunningham of Lanbroughton.. [NRS.GD149.332]

CUNNINGHAM, JOHN, in Leiden, Holland, a letter, 1689. [NRS.RH15.106.677]

CUNNINGHAM, JOHN, a soldier, near Brussels, 1693. [NRS.GD26.13.424]

CUNNINGHAM, ROBERT, formerly a drummer with a Scottish regiment in the Low Countries, was appointed town drummer of Aberdeen on 12 February 1623. [Aberdeen Burgh Council Register]

CUNNINGHAM, THOMAS, factor in Veere, Zealand, 1641. [SHS.6/3]

CURRY, PETER, a Scottish seaman under Captain Engelbrecht Pieters van der Zee, and his wife Lysbeth Jans living on the house of Cornelis Pieters a bricklayer on the livestock market, testament, 7 November 1639. [GAR.ONA.113.50.77]

CUTLER, ROBERT, from Edinburgh, and Anna Jans in Rotterdam, were married in Rotterdam on 28 November 1655. [GAR]

DALGLEISH, GEORGE, from Culross, Fife, married Janet Strachan, from Rotterdam, in the Scots Kirk in Rotterdam on 13 October 1720. [GAR]

DALRYMPLE, DAVID, a shipmaster in V

eere, Zealand, skipper of the Anne of Kirkcaldy, testament, 1692, Commissariat of St Andrews. [NRS]

DALZIELL, ALEXANDER, was granted a pass to travel from England to Holland on 4 June 1706. [TNA.SP44.393.2]

DALZELL, JOHN, in Ostende, Flanders a letter, 1696. [NRS.GD30.2003]

DAVID, JOHN, son of James David in Balmerino, Fife, married Elizabeth Watson, widow of J. Hamilton, in the Scots Kirk in Rotterdam on 31 March 1740. [GAR]

DAVIDSEN, ARNT, from Aberdeen, a cramer who was admitted as a burgess of Antwerpen, Flanders, in 1598. [SAA]

DAVIDSON, GEORGE, a Scottish cobbler, and his wife Stijntge Jansdochter, testament, 12 February 1636. [GAR.ONA.196.23.40]

DAVIDSON, JOHN, from Edinburgh, married Marritgen Joosten, in Rotterdam on 22 March 1626. [GAR]

DAVIDSON, JOHN, from Edinburgh, married Janettie Robberts, from Rotterdam, in Rotterdam on 22 February 1695. [GAR]

DAVIDSON, JOHN, from Bo'ness, West Lothian, married Josyntje Jacobs, from Rotterdam, in the Scots Kirk in Rotterdam on 22 May 1708. [GAR]

DAVIDSON, JOHN, from Aberdeen, was admitted as a citizen of Rotterdam in 1739. [GAR]

DAVISON, MARJORIE, relict of late George Corstor sometime factor at Veere, Zealand, now spouse to George Riddell in Veere, 1633. [SHS.6/3]

DAVIDSON, MAGNUS, born in Scotland, bound for Greenland, testament, 2 May 1619, refers to Anna Jansdochter wife of Willem Janszoon. [GAR.ONA.37/85]

DAVIDSON, PETER, a merchant in Amsterdam in 1720. [GAA.NA.8571.1189]

DAVIDSON, ROBERT, a Scotsman, husband of Aeltghen Doubles,a seaman aboard the Dordrecht bound for the West Indies, testament, 17 April 1629. [GAR.ONA.186.23.43]

DAVIDSON, ROBERT, from Scotland, was admitted as a citizen of Rotterdam in 1739. [GAR]

DAVIDSON, SYMON, master of the Palm of Hoorn which arrived in the Clyde from La Rochelle, France, in April 1627; also on 10 August 1627. [GBR]

DAVIDSON, WILLIAM, a merchant in Amsterdam, 23 July 1745. [GAA.NA.12320/S4]

DAVIDSON, WILLIAM, born 1713, son of Reverend Thomas Davidson and his wife Janet Rodger, a merchant in Rotterdam, died 20 September 1794. [F.5.316]; a merchant in Rotterdam, was granted the lands of Muirhouse on 24 February 1777. [NAS.RGSS.117/214]; in Rotterdam, testament, sasine, 24.3.1777, Edinburgh. [NRS.RS27.232.40]

DAWSON, JAMES, an elder of the Scots Church in Rotterdam, 1653-1656. [GAR]

DE COE, ROETOF CORNELIUS, master of the Young Francis of Rotterdam, from Aberdeen to Zurick Zee on 12 September 1746. [NRS.E504.1.2]

DE GRAVE, CLAUDE, merchant in Haarlem, Holland, appointed Walter Hamilton, merchant burgess of Edinburgh, as his factor, 15 November 1659. [ECA.MBII.42/1759]

DE GRAVE, PEITER, son of Claud de Grave a merchant in Haarlem, Holland, a deed of factory, 20 August 1661. [NRS.RD2.2.255]

DE MULLINDER, FRANCIS, a merchant in Brugge, Flanders, in 1686. [NRS.AC7]

DENNISTON, ROBERT, was appointed as Conservator of the Scots Privileges at Veere, Zealand, in 1589. [SSV.186]

DE POTTER, SOPHIA, widow of Cornelius Ball, merchant in Haarlem, Holland, appointed Walter Hamilton, merchant burgess of Edinburgh, as her factor, 15 November 1659. [ECA.MBII.42/1759]

DEVOSE, BARNET, a soap-maker in Rotterdam, testament, 25 April 1666, Comm. Edinburgh. [NRS]

DE JONG, CRYN, master of the Juffrow Willemina, trading between Rotterdam and Perth in 1764. [NRS.E504.27.4]

DE VOS, JAN, a Dutch harpooner aboard the Peggy of Glasgow whaling off Greenland in 1751. [NRS.E508.48.8]

DICKSON, ALEXANDER, a Scot, was married in Bergen op Zoom, Brabant, on 14 November 1636. [WBA]

DICK, ANDREW, from Largo in Fife, married Sara de Bruyn, from Rotterdam, in Rotterdam on 11 October 1740. [GAR] , was admitted as a citizen of Rotterdam in 1740. [GAR]

DICKSON, JOHN, a Scotsman, aboard the Dordrecht bound for the West Indies, a testament, 10 April 1628, refers to

William Johnston, a Scots, living in St George's Lane, Rotterdam. [GAR.ONA.128/178/488]

DICKSON, LOUIS, from Edinburgh, married Jaquelyne Willems, from Arnhem, Gelderland, in Rotterdam on 8 October 1606. [GAR]

DIRCKSON, ADAM, son of Adam Dirckson in Kilmarnock, Ayrshire, married Margaret ....., in the Scots Kirk in Rotterdam on 11 September 1715. [GAR]

DIXON, JOHN, the younger, son of John Dixon in Edinburgh, was apprenticed to Martin van Halewijn a shopkeeper in Amsterdam, for three years, in 1624. [GAA.170/120]

DIXON, JOHN, from Glasgow, married Barbara Tapes, in the Scots Kirk in Rotterdam on 27 October 1717. [GAR]

DIXON, ROBERT, a servant, was granted a pass to travel from England to Holland on 24 September 1706. [TNA.SP44.393.98]

DOCTOR, MAISIE, in Vlissingen, Zealand, wife of Robert Angus a shipmaster in Burntisland, Fife, who was bound on a voyage to the West Indies in 1643. [NRS.GD172.293]

DON, JOHN, a Scot, was married in Bergen op Zoom, Brabant, on 14 April 1734. [WBA]

DONALDSON, JOHN, from Aberdeen, married Elizabeth Crookshanks, in the Scots Kirk in Rotterdam on 13 July 1724. [GAR]

DONALDSON, WILLIAM, from Leith, Midlothian, a Scots sailor bound for the West Indies aboard the ship Utrecht master Cornelis Claeszoon 't Meickmeijsgen, testament, 4 May 1629, refers to John Garner. [GAR.ONA.189.129.206]

DOUGALL, THOMAS, a Scot, was married in Bergen op Zoom, Brabant, on 17 December 1718. [WBA]

DOUGLAS, ALEXANDER, from Culross, Fife, was admitted as a citizen of Rotterdam on 14 December 1719. [GAR]

DOUGLAS, HUGH, son of Robert Douglas a merchant in Leith, Midlothian, a sailor aboard the James of Dundee bound for Virginia, absconded and enlisted in Marjorybanks' regiment in the service of Holland, 1748. [NRS.AC10.339]

DOUGLAS, JAMES, was granted a pass to travel from England to Holland on 4 July 1706. [TNA.SP44.393.23]

DOUGLAS, JOHN, witnessed a deed in Amsterdam in 1629. [NRS.GD84.2.177]

DOUGLAS, ROBERT, from Edinburgh, was married in Bergen op Zoom, Brabant, on 26 June 1754. [WBA]

DOUGLAS, WILLIAM, from Edinburgh, was admitted as a citizen of Rotterdam on 5 August 1716. [GAR]

DOW, JOHN, a Scot, was married in Bergen op Zoom, Brabant, on 23 March 1707. [WBA]

DOWIE, JOHN, from Lundin in Fife, married Margery Naughton, in the Scots Kirk in Rotterdam on 24 April 1774. [GAR]

DREDAN, THOMAS, an elder of the Scots Church in Rotterdam, 1648-1650. [GAR]

DRUMMOND, DAVID, factor at Veere, Zealand, 1634. [SHS.6/3]

DRUMMOND, JOHN, of Quarrell, a merchant in Amsterdam and London, letters, 1700-1734 Trading with William Pringle, a merchant in Surinam, letters 1700-1725.. [NRS.GD24.1.464D]

DRUMMOND, PATRICK, Conservator of the Scottish Privileges at Veere, Zealand, 1633. [SHS/6/3]

DRUMMOND, WILLIAM, a tailor, was admitted as a burgess of Antwerpen, Flanders, in 1537. [SAA]

DRUMMOND, Sir WILLIAM, Colonel of a Scots regiment in the service of the States General of Holland, a commission, 1646. [NRAS.1100.1628]

DRUMMOND, WILLIAM, from Bo'ness, West Lothian, was admitted as a citizen of Rotterdam in 1747. [GAR]

DUGUID, GEORGE, born 1783, died on Orangestein Estate, Essequibo, on 7 January, 1807. [SM.69.798]

DUNCAN, ALEXANDER, from Dysart, Fife, was admitted as a citizen of Rotterdam in 1740. [GAR]

DUNCAN, ADAM, a merchant in Rotterdam, deeds,1715, [NRS.RD3.144.198; RD3.145.553, 768; RD3.146.1, 41]; 1730s. [NRS.CSB59.37.8.13]; trading with James McMichael in Perth, in 1717. [NRS.B59.37.8.2]; from Dundee, was admitted as a citizen of Rotterdam in 1730. [GAR]; dead by 1738, uncle of Alexander Duncan of Lundie in Angus. [NRS.S/H]

DUNCAN, ADAM, a merchant in Rotterdam, 1798. [NRS.CS17.1.16/388]

DUNCAN, ARCHIBALD, was granted a pass to travel from England to Holland on 24 September 1706. [TNA.SP44.393.98]

DUNCAN, GIDEON, in Ostend, Flanders,1792. [NRAS.3955.60.1.191]

DUNCAN, JAMES, from Crail, Fife, married Margaret Carlyle from Cramond, Midlothian, in the Scots Kirk in Rotterdam on 11 April 1708. [GAR]

DUNCAN, THOMAS, from Edinburgh, married Tanneken Jans, from Breda, Brabant, in Rotterdam on 2 August 1598. [GAR]

DUNCAN, WILLIAM, a merchant in Berbice, died on 21 April 1814. [EC.6211]

DUND, [?], JOHN, from Dundee, was admitted as a citizen of Rotterdam in 1747. [GAR]

DUNDAS, JAMES, Lieutenant Colonel of Colonel Gordon's Regiment in the service of the States General, died in Maastricht, Limburg, on 15 December 1761. [SM.24.55]

DUNDAS, WILLIAM, in Rotterdam and Leiden, Holland,1716. [NRS.GD1.616.44]; in Rotterdam, a letter, 1716, [NRS.GD30.1564]; in Utrecht, a letter, 1723. [NRS.GD158.1300]

DUNHAM, DAVID, from Carriden, West Lothian, married Janet Provan, in the Scots Kirk in Rotterdam in September 1723. [GAR]

DUNLOP, DAVID, from Fenwick in Ayrshire, married Janet Robert, in the Scots Kirk in Rotterdam on 2 June 1753. [GAR]; was admitted as a citizen of Rotterdam in 1755. [GAR]

DUNLOP, JAMES, an elder of the Scots Church in Rotterdam, 1687-1689. [GAR]

DUNN, JOHN, son of David Dunn in Kilconquhar in Fife, married Helen Wilson, widow of Rodger Mowat, in the Scots Kirk in Rotterdam on 6 October 1719. [GAR]

DURIE, JAMES, a merchant and an assessor of the Scots Court in Veere, Zealand, in 1735. [NRS.RH11.2.1]

DURIS, ['JOORIS'], THOMAS, from Edinburgh, a laborer in Veere, Zealand, an inventory, 1559. [GAV.Invenrory.920]

DURKIE, ALEXANDER, from Dysart in Fife, married Katherine Palmer, daughter of James in Edinburgh, in the Scots Kirk in Rotterdam on 26 September 1767. [GAR]

ECHLIN, HENRY, grandson of Henry Echlin of Pittadro, a soldier in Flanders, 1623. [NRS.GD172.114]

EDMOND, JOHN, from Stirling, a seaman aboard the ship New Rotterdam bound for the East Indies, testament, 14 December 1643, refers to his brothers and sisters living in Stirling – William Edmond, Robert Edmond, Margaret Edmond, Janet Edmond, and Elizabeth Edmond. [GAR.ONA.205.150.207]

EDMONSTON, DAVID, M.A., an elder of the Scots Church in Rotterdam, 1693-1714. [GAR]

EDMONSTONE, JOHN, a young Scotsman, a seaman under Captain Jan van Nes, testament, 26 August 1641, refers to Elisabeth Duncan widow of John Smith, mother of John Smith the young Scots seaman, living on the Schiedam dyke in Rotterdam. [GAR.ONA.202.224.285]

EDY, DAVID, from Lerwick in the Shetland Islands, married Catherine MacAlaster, in the Scots Kirk in Rotterdam on 13 December 1758. [GAR]

EDY, JAMES, from Bo'ness, West Lothian, married Janet Grant, in the Scots Kirk in Rotterdam on 16 August 1747. [GAR]

EDY, WILLIAM ADAMSON, from Bo'ness, West Lothian, was admitted as a citizen of Rotterdam in 1744. [GAR]

EIDISON, JAN, master of the Waterdog of Enschede arrived in the Clyde on 1 June 1627. [GBR]

ELES, JAMES, factor in Veere, Zealand, 1641, a letter, 1643. [SHS.6/3][NRS.GD18.24.34]

ELGIN, GEORGE, from Berwick-on-Tweed, was admitted as a citizen of Rotterdam in 1754. [GAR];married Francine Aalmis from Rotterdam, in the Scots Kirk in Rotterdam on 23 November 1755. [GAR].

ELLIOT, ROBERT, in Demerara, a will dated May 1779. [NRS.RD4.235.748]

ELLIOT ["ALLIOD"], THOMAS, graduated from Leiden University, Holland, in 1746. [UL]

ELLIS, THOMAS, from Aberdeen, recruited for service in the Dutch West Indies, 17 March 1640. [GAA.NA926/97]

EMONDORFF, ..., an apothecary in Maastricht, Limburg, a letter, 1693. [NAS.GD1.885.19]

ERSKINE, HARRY, in Breda, Brabant, a letter, 1702. [NRS.GD124.15.220]

ERSKINE, JAMES, in Utrecht, an account, 1702. [NRS.GD45.17.815]

EVANSON, ROBERT, from Leith, Midlothian, was admitted as a citizen of Rotterdam on 11 August 1718. [GAR]

EWIN, ALEXANDER, a factor in Veere, Zealand, and master of the Concergerie house there before 1613. [SSN.147]

EWING, THOMAS, reader in the Scots Kirk at Veere, Zealand, in 1614. [SSV.274]

FAA, JOHN, an elder of the Scots Church in Rotterdam, 1687-1706. [GAR]

FAIRBAIRN, PETER, died in Berbice on 10 June 1822. [BM.12.519]

FAIRHOLM, ANDREW, from Edinburgh, was admitted as a citizen of Rotterdam in 1739. [GAR]

FAIRHOLM, WILLIAM, from Edinburgh, was admitted as a citizen of Rotterdam in 1766. [GAR]; late merchant in Rotterdam, was granted the lands of St John's Chapel on 6 August 1783. [NRS.RGSS.121/266]

FAIRLAY, ADAM, a Scotsman from Glasgow, a servant of Captain Leendert Adryaenszoon Haexhwant, testament, refers to William Johnston a Scotsman. [GAR.ONA.128.309.810]

FALCONER, ROBERT, in Rotterdam, a sasine, 1701. [NRS.RH8.1344]

FARQUHARSON, ANDREW, in Demerara in 1796. [NRS.RH1.852]

FENTON, HENRY, from the Shetland Islands, married Martha Robertson from the Shetland Islands, in the Scots Kirk in Rotterdam on 16 February 1763. [GAR]

FERGUSON, GEORGE, a Scot, was married in Bergen op Zoom, Zealand, on 3 May 1628. [WBA]

FERGUSON, JAMES, a Scot, was married in Bergen op Zoom, Zealand, on 3 October 1634. [WBA]

FERGUSON JAMES, a servant, was granted a pass to travel from England to Holland on 5 April 1706. [TNA.SP44.390.415a]

FERGUSON, JOHN, from Dunoon, Argyll, a soldier aboard the Achillies bound for the East Indies, testament, 28 March 1659, refers to his wife Margaret Aird in Scotland. [GAR.ONA.217.78.285]

FERGUSON, JOHN, son of John Ferguson in Falkirk, Stirlingshire, married Mary Van Der Leer, in the Scots Kirk in Rotterdam on 25 March 1711. [GAR]

FERGUSON, JOHN, from Minniburgh, [Monyabroch?], married Margaret Arthur from Rotterdam, in the Scots Kirk in Rotterdam on 28 November 1768, witnesses were John Murray and Alexander Cassills. [GAR]

FERGUSON, JOHN, late in Essequibo, now in Stranraer, Wigtownshire, 1821. [NRS.CS17.1.40.393]; Testament, 29 October 1821, Commissariot Wigtown. [NRS]

FERGUSON, WALTER, from Aberdeenshire, was admitted as a citizen of Rotterdam in 1720. [GAR]

FERGUSON, WILLIAM, from Glasgow, married Mary Bryan from Yarmouth, England, in Rotterdam on 20 June 1768. [GAR]

FERGUSON, WILLIAM, from Leith, Midlothian, married Ann Boogey from South Shields, England, in the Scots Kirk in Rotterdam on 2 March 1777. [GAR]

FERRIER, Colonel HAY, in the service of the States of Holland, before 1782. [NRS.CS17.1.1/41][NRAS.4159.10.1]

FERRIER, JOHN, from Bo'ness, West Lothian, was admitted as a citizen of Rotterdam on 11 September 1714. [GAR]

FETTES, ALEXANDER, from Aberdeen, was admitted as a citizen of Rotterdam on 20 September 1720. [GAR]

FINLASON, JAMES, was granted a pass to travel from England to Holland on 18 June 1706. [TNA.SP44.393.18]

FINLAYSON, JOHN, from Stirling, a soldier aboard the New Rotterdam master Jocchum Claeszoon, bound for the East Indies, testament, 27 March 1657, refers to William Williamson, a Scotsman, and his wife Maddeleentge Abramsdochter, and his mother Barbara Jackson widow of James Finlayson from Stirling, also his brother William Finlayson in Stirling. [GAR.ONA.216.60.223], see also [GAR.ONA.216.59.221]

FINLASON, JOHN, a mariner aboard the Unity of Aberdeen, a witness before the Scots Court in Veere, Zealand, in 1739. [NRS.RH11.2.1]

FLETCHER, ..., was born in Berbice on 14 December 1805. [SM.68.155]

FLINT, JAMES, in Middelburg, Zealand, a letter, 1618. [NRS.RH9.2.100]

FISSIE, JOHN, master of the George of Queensferry, died in Holland, 1696. [NRS.AC9.429]

FLEMING, JOHN, a factor in Holland, 1676. [NRS.AC7.2]

FLEMING, JOHN, from Dysart in Fife, married Elizabeth Warran from Linlithgow, in the Scots Kirk in Rotterdam on 21 February 1733. [GAR]

FLEMING, JOHN, a mariner in Rotterdam, eldest son of Andrew Fleming a burgess of Dysart, Fife, a deed, 1773. [NRS.B21.5.2.205]

FLEMING, ROBERT, minister of the Scots Church in Rotterdam, a letter, 1692. [NRS.GD26.13.243]

FLEMING, ROBERT, from Linlithgow, West Lothian, married Margriet Logge, in the Scots Kirk in Rotterdam on 6 March 1708. [GAR]

FLEMING, THOMAS, an elder of the Scots Church in Rotterdam, 1650. [GAR]

FLETCHER, H., in Breda, Brabant, a letter, 1682.
[NRS.GD406.1.3141.2]

FLETCHER, ROBERT, from Dundee, was admitted as a
citizen of Rotterdam on 31 July 1716. [GAR]

FLUCKER, DAVID, from Lasswade, Midlothian, a gunner
aboard the Den Cleynen Erasmus, master Jan Pieterszoon,
bound for the East Indies, testament, 12 April 1622, refers to
his wife Liesbeth Pieterszoon Van Ceulen.
[GAR.ONA.103/120/205]

FORBES, ALEXANDER, a Scot, was married in Bergen op
Zoom, Brabant, on 24 July 1720. [WBA]

FORBES, GEORGE, a factor, married Susan, Countess
Dowager of Strathmore, in 1745, parents of Susan Amelia
Forbes born 17 May 1746 in Rotterdam. Process of declaratory
of marriage, July 1756. [NRS.CC8.6.363]

FORBES, JOHN, from Aberdeen, a quartermaster under Vice
Admiral Jasper Adriaenzoon Liefhebber on the ship 't Zeecalf,
testament, 30 June 1629, refers to Steven Gerritszoon
Blindeman and his wife Magdelana Belang.
[GAR.ONA.189.155.255]

FORBES, JOHN, brother of Patrick Forbes the Bishop of
Aberdeen, a minister in Middelburg, Zealand, was admitted as
a burgess of Aberdeen 1 August 1619. [ABR]

FORBES, JOHN, from Cupar in Fife, married Janet Thomson
from Rotterdam, in the Scots Kirk in Rotterdam on 20 July
1712. [GAR]

FORBES, JOHN, from Aberdeen, was admitted as a citizen of
Rotterdam in 1749. [GAR];in Rotterdam, 1755.
[NRAS.332/C3/1335-1387]

FORBES, WILLIAM, from Aberdeen, married Elizabeth
Jacobs from Rotterdam, in Rotterdam on 27 December 1707.
[GAR]

FORDYCE, JAMES, servant to the Marquis of Tullibardine, was granted a pass travel from England to Holland on 3 December 1705. [TNA.SP44.390.341]

FORDYCE, JAMES, from the Shetland Islands, married Elizabeth Mudie from the Shetland Islands, in the Scots Kirk in Rotterdam on 18 June 1746. [GAR]

FORGAN, ROBERT, an elder of the Scots Church in Rotterdam, 1650-1653. [GAR]

FORREST, JAMES, from Edinburgh, married Christine Ramsay from Dysart, Fife, in the Scots Kirk in Rotterdam on 22 December 1736. [GAR]; was admitted as a citizen of Rotterdam on 14 October 1719. [GAR]

FORREST, WILLIAM, from Scotland, was admitted as a citizen of Rotterdam in 1756. [GAR]

FORRESTER, ANDREW, from Edinburgh, married Jannetje Livingston from Rotterdam, in the Scots Kirk in Rotterdam on 9 March 1740. [GAR]

FORRET, JOHN, minister at Newburn in Fife, was appointed as minister of the Scots Kirk in Veere, Zealand, in 1627, he died by 1630. [SSV.277]

FORRET, Sir WILLIAM, Captain of Lancers in the service of Flanders, died 1600. [St Walburgaskerk, MI, Brugge]

FORSTER, JOHN, a merchant from Leith, Midlothian, was admitted as a burger of Antwerpen, Flanders, in 1537. [SAA]

FORSYTH, ALEXANDER, from Huntly, Aberdeenshire, was admitted as a citizen of Rotterdam in 1774. [GAR]

FOSTER, JAMES, from St Ninians, Stirlingshire, married Isobel Carlisle from Cramond West Lothian, in the Scots Kirk in Rotterdam on 2 February 1707. [GAR]

FOTHERINGHAM, NORMAN, from Culross, Fife, married Janet Kelck from Rotterdam, in the Scots Kirk in Rotterdam on 5 May 1717. [GAR]

FOTHERINGHAM, ROBERT, from Culross, Fife, married Jannetje Hendricks van Casteel from Rotterdam, in the Scots Kirk in Rotterdam on 1 November 1679. [GAR]

FOTHERINGHAM, THOMAS, from Scotland, , was admitted as a citizen of Rotterdam in 1754. [GAR]

FRANCK, ALEXANDER, son of John Franck an advocate in Edinburgh, married Agnes Davidson, in the Scots Kirk in Rotterdam on 29 June 1707, witnesses were James Forrester, a skipper, and Alexander Melvill. [GAR]

FRANK, CHARLES, of Boughtbridge, Captain of the Scots Brigade in the service of the States of Holland, born 1743, died 1791. [Eccles MI, Berwickshire]

FRASER, or FRISSELL, ALEXANDER, a Captain born in Lovat, Inverness-shire, living in Den Haag, testaments, 21 March 1626, refers to Andrew Fraser in Inverness. 16 June 1628. [GAR.ONA.128.81.217; 128.196.522]

FRAZER, ALEXANDER, an Episcopalian chaplain to Colonel Hamilton's regiment in the Netherlands, stationed in Veere, Zealand, in 1701. [SSV.315]

FRASER, DAVID, from Dundee, was admitted as a citizen of Rotterdam in 1752. [GAR]

FRASER, DONALD, son of Alexander Fraser in Inverness-shire, married Mary McEwan, daughter of John McEwan in Bergen-op-Zoom, in the Scots Kirk in Rotterdam on 6 September 1719. [GAR]

FRASER, GILBERT, a merchant in Edinburgh, testament, 4 December 1639, refers to Sara Barents daughter of his late sister Janet Fraser and her spouse Richard Barents. [GAR.ONA.327.311.688]

FRASER, JAMES, the younger of Belladrum, Inverness-shire, purchased an estate in Dutch Demerara in 1790. [NRS.HCA.D238.D1.17/6] [possibly the Colchester Plantation in Berbice]

FRASER, JAMES, in Berbice, probate PCC 15 August 1801. [TNA]

FRASER, JOHN DANIEL, from the Shetland Islands, married Lena Tanson from Rotterdam on 4 September 1708. [GAR]

FRASER, MALCOLM, of Culduthel, Inverness-shire, late Captain in Lord John Murray's Regiment of Foot, died in Bergen-op-Zoom on 27 July 1747. [NRS.CC8.6.340]

FRASER, SIMON, eldest son of Donald Fraser of Balloan, of the Golden Fleece Plantation in Berbice, died there on 15 September 1803. [DPCA.72]

FRASER, SUSAN, eldest daughter of Simon Fraser of Kilmorack, married M.Katz in Berbice on 9 January 1826. [EA]

FRASER, WILLIAM, a Scot, was married in Bergen op Zoom, Zealand, on 5 January 1746. [WBA]

FRASER, WILLIAM, a planter in Berbice in 1818. [NRS.CS96.2130.1]

FREIS, MINART, a Dutchman, and Janet Whitehead or Hay, parents of Minart and David, born in Leith, Midlothian, before 1570. [NRS.CC8.2.4.330]

FRISELL, JEREMY, from the Shetland Islands, married Lysbet Isaacx from Dordrecht, Holland, in Delfshaven on 18 January 1668. [GAR]

GAIRN, JAMES, a Scotsman, a seaman under Captain Flips Schoneman, testament, 26 August 1641, refers to Francis Cochrane, a Scotsman, and his spouse Anneken Andriesdochter. [GAR.ONA.202.223.284]

GAIRNS, JAMES, a mariner aboard the Unity of Aberdeen, a witness before the Scots Court in Veere, Zealand, in 1739. [NRS.RH11.2.1]

GARNER, JOHN, son of James Garner in Bo'ness, West Lothian, married Elisabeth Rodger widow of John Mirkle who died by falling overboard in Amsterdam, in the Scots Kirk in Rotterdam in 1701. [GAR]

GAVIN, ALEXANDER, from Montrose, Angus, was admitted as a citizen of Rotterdam in 1746. [GAR]

GAVIN, DAVID, a merchant in Middleburg, was granted the lands of Easter Braikie in Angus on 6 August 1753. [NRS.RGSS.102/83]; and his wife Christina Maria Heansy in Middleburg in 1751. [NRAS.2238.2.23]; papers, 1747-1757, [NRAS.2236.2.4; NRAS2238.2.19]

GAVIN, JOHN, son of George Gavin in Queensferry, West Lothian, and Maty Hay in Rotterdam, were married in the Scots Kirk in Rotterdam on 12 September 1733. [GAR]

GAVIN, JOSEPH, merchant in Middleburg, Holland, died 25 July 1770. [NRS.CS97.110.20]

GAVIN and GREGORY, merchants in Veere, accounts, 1758. [NRAS.2236.3.5]

GAY, ALEXANDER, son of John Gay in Greenock, Renfrewshire, and Margaret Nietter in Dalmahoy, were married in the Scots Kirk in Rotterdam 30 November 1707. [GAR] , was admitted as a citizen of Rotterdam in 1720. [GAR]

GAY, ALEXANDER, from Glasgow, and Marytje Lavestein in Delftshaven, were married in Rotterdam on 13 September 1718. [GAR]; was admitted as a citizen of Rotterdam on 7 October 1720. [GAR]

GAY, JACOB, from Glasgow, and Jennetje Stuart in Rotterdam, were married in Rotterdam on 27 September 1726. [GAR]

GEDDES, DAVID, in Bergen op den Zoom, Brabant, son of Robert Gordon of Scotstoun, a letter, 17 October 1733. [NRS.RH15.70.26]

GEEN, CORNELIS, a doctor in Vlissingen, Zealand, 1742. [NRS.AC9.1522]

GEEN, MARINUS, a doctor in Vlissingen, Zealand, 1742. [NRS.AC9.1522]

GEORGE, ANDREW, from Leith, Midlothian, a soldier under E. Der Bout, married Francyn Tennis from Rotterdam, in Rotterdam on 1 March 1587. [GAR]

GEORGE, JOHN, from Aberdeen, and Elizabeth Andress from Banff, were married in the Scots Kirk in Rotterdam on 1 July 1761. [GAR]

GEORGESON, PETER, born in Scotland, a seaman under Captain Chritaen Elderszoon, testament, 25 February 1666, refers to Corstiaen and Fijtge Claes. [GAR.ONA.363.149.511]

GERRY, JAMES, from Glasgow, married Elisabeth Morgan widow of Thomas Waters in Dublin, were married in Rotterdam on 15 January 1733. [GAR]

'GHES', [Gass?], JOHN, a Scottish steward, testament, 3 January 1633, refers to Marion Baebson a Scot, his future wife, and Captain Jan van Nesch. [GAR.ONA.42.224.352]

GIB, ROBERT, an elder of the Scots Church in Rotterdam, 1683-1686. [GAR]

GIBBON, ROBERT, from Aberdeen, was admitted as a citizen of Rotterdam in 1770. [GAR]

GIBSON, GEORGE, from Paisley, Renfrewshire, and Janet Hardie from Bo'ness, West Lothian, were married in the Scots Kirk in Rotterdam on 24 June 1767. [GAR]; was admitted as a citizen of Rotterdam in 1767. [GAR]

GIBSON, JAMES, from Bo'ness, West Lothian, a seaman under Captain Pieter Janszoon van den Brouck, testament, 26 February 1644, refers to James Robertson and his wife Greta Scott living near the fish market in Rotterdam. [GAR.ONA.205.265.355]

GIBSON, JAMES, from 'Bouhartpans', was admitted as a citizen of Rotterdam on 19 September 1718. [GAR]

GIBSON, JOHN, from Lanark, and Josyntje Norrie from Bo'ness, West Lothian, were married in Rotterdam on 5 June 1708. [GAR]

GIBSON, JOHN, from Bo'ness, West Lothian, and Isabella Auckworth from Sunderland, England, were married in the Scots Kirk in Rotterdam on 31 May 1788. [GAR]

GIBSON, WILLIAM, from Aberdeen, and Barbara Yeats in Rotterdam, were married in the Scots Kirk in Rotterdam on 5 August 1769.[GAR]

GIBSON, WILLIAM, from Westhall, was admitted as a citizen of Rotterdam on 11 January 1720. [GAR]

GILBERT, GILBERT, from Aberdeen, a young man, a corporal under Captain Huybert Jacob Huygen, aboard the Gorcum, testament, 15 February 1666.
[GAR.ONA.223.100.348]; Also he as an upper corporal under Lieutenant Admiral Aert Janszoon van Nes, testament, 1 April 1667, refers to Elizabeth Rin, widow of Gilbert Alcorn living in Leuvehaven. [GAR.ONA.224.77.293]

GILCHRIST, JAMES, a young Scotsman, a seaman under Captain Corstiaen Eldertszoon aboard the Gorcum, testament, 28 September 1653, refers to his comrade William Johnson a young Scotsman. [GAR.ONA.214.104.307]

GILLON, ALEXANDER, from Bo'ness, West Lothian, was admitted as a citizen of Rotterdam in 1740. [GAR]

GILLYES, ALEXANDER, was granted a pass to travel from England to Holland on 25 October 1705. [TNA.SP44.391.182]

GILMOUR, GEORGE, was bound for West Flanders to be educated in 1642. [NRS.GD122.2.559-560]

GLASFORD, DUNCAN, from Bo'ness West Lothian, wss admitted as a citizen of Rotterdam on 23 April 1710. [GAR]

GLOVER, JOHN, from Cupar, wss admitted as a citizen of Rotterdam on 26 March 1710. [GAR]

GLEN, JAMES, from Bo'ness, West Lothian, and Janet Tate in Rotterdam, were married in Rotterdam on 31 May 1705. [GAR]

GLEN, JOHN, a Scotsman, sailor under Captain Robert Post, testament, 15 March 1638, refers to his uncle Thomas Henderson living in Rotterdam. [GAR.ONA.197.381.464]

GLEN, THOMAS, from Queensferry, West Lothian, a seaman aboard the ship New Rotterdam bound for the East Indies, testament, 15 December 1643, refers to his brother William Glen and his sister Elisabeth Glen, to James Roon and his wife Margaret Blackadder living on the Schiedam dyke. [GAR.ONA.205.157.217]

GLENNIE, DAVID, a Scottish laborer in Veere, Zealand, an inventory, 1533. [GAV.Inv.920]

GOODLAD, THOMAS, son of Matthew Goodlad in Lerwick, the Shetland Islands, and Helen Hamilton also from Lerwick, were married in the Scots Kirk in Rotterdam oin 7 August 1765. [GAR]

GORDON, ALEXANDER, a Scot from 'Carrenborre', a seaman under Captain Willem Joosten van Colster, testament, 21 November 1629, refers to William Watson. [GAR.ONA.190.12.17]

GORDON, ALEXANDER, a merchant in Amsterdam, heir to his father Robert Gordon of Cairnfield, 10 May 1718. [NRS.S/H]

GORDON, ALEXANDER, a merchant in Amsterdam, 23 July 1745. [GAA.NA.12320/S4]

GORDON, CHARLES, minister of the Scots kirk in Veere Zealand, from 1686 until 1691. [SSV.304-305]

GORDON, CHARLES, of Kirdells, a Captain of Colonel Lauder's Regiment in Flanders, 1694. [NRS.CC8.6.67]

GORDON, GEORGE, Conservator of the Scots Privileges at Veere, Zealand, from 1553 to 1555, and from 1561 to 1565. [SSV.171]

GORDON, GEORGE, President of the Court of Justice in Berbice, died there on 15 November 1820. [BM.9.708]

GORDON, JAMES, an elder of the Scots Church in Rotterdam, 1678-1684. [GAR]

GORDON, JAMES, a merchant in Amsterdam, a charter party with Alexander Jollie, master of the James of Prestonpans, for a voyage from Rotterdam to Aberdeen in 1681. [NRS.RH9.17.32/14]

GORDON, JAMES, of Craiglaw, a soldier in Holland, a diary, 1710-1712. [NRAS.275.3.2]

GORDON, JAMES, from Carmichael, Lanarkshire, and Margaret Wark from Glasgow, were married in the Scots Kirk in Rotterdam on 1 November 1736. [GAR]

GORDON, JOHN, in Rotterdam, a letter, 1678. [NRS.GD1.885.9]

GORDON, JOHN, an elder of the Scots Church in Rotterdam, 1694-1697. [GAR]

GORDON, JOHN, son of George Gordon in Banff, and Jean Gordon, daughter of John Gordon of Barwick, Fochabers, were married in the Scots Kirk in Rotterdam on 2 June 1706. [GAR]

GORDON, JOHN, was granted a pass to travel from England to Holland on 21 September 1706. [TNA.SP44.393.91]

GORDON, JOHN, from 'Grenser' in Scotland, and Antonetta Hensius from Den Haag, were married in Rotterdam on 3 October 1723. [GAR]

GORDON, JOHN, son of Sir William Gordon of Invergordon, Ross and Cromarty, a witness in Utrecht, 1724. [NRS.GD84.1.33.1]

GORDON, PETER, of Plantation Borlum, Berbice, dead by 1809. [NRS.GD23.7.39]

GORDON, ROBERT, from Aberdeen, and Elisabeth Okey from Southwold, England, were married in Rotterdam on 25

August 1735. [GAR]; was admitted as a citizen of Rotterdam in 1735. [GAR]

GORDON, THOMAS, from Aberdeen, was admitted as a citizen of Rotterdam on 9 December 1711. [GAR]

GORDON, THOMAS a Scot, was married in Bergen-op-Zoom on 13 November 1733. [WBA]

GORDON, WILLIAM, a servant, was granted a pass to travel from England to Holland on 5 April 1706. [TNA.SP44.390.415a]

GORDON, WILLIAM, of Craichlaw, in Holland, letters, 1711-1712. [NRAS.275.4.1]

GORDON, ..., a merchant from Aberdeen, was appointed as an assessor of the Scots Court in Veere, Zealand, in 1738. [NRS.RH11.2.1]

GORIS, SEGERUS, MA, son of Trelimani Goris a merchant in Rotterdam, was admitted as a guilds-brother of Aberdeen on 8 July 1678. [ABR]

GOURLAY, JAMES, a Scot, was married in Bergen op Zoom, Zealand, on 17 August 1649. [WBA]

GOVAN, JOHN, from Carriden, West Lothian, and Margaret Higgens in Rotterdam, were married in the Scots Kirk in Rotterdam on 10 October 1744. [GAR]

GOWAN, DAVID, from Scotland, was admitted as a citizen of Rotterdam in 1771. [GAR]

GRAHAM, ANNE, and her daughter **MARGARET,** were granted a pass to travel from England to Holland on 6 April 1706. [TNA.SP44.390.423]

GRAHAM, JAMES, a Scot, was married in Bergen op Zoom, Zealand, on 15 August 1714. [WBA]

GRAHAM, JOHN, from Leven, Fife, and Helen Mack, daughter of James Mack, were married in the Scots Kirk in Rotterdam on 1 May 1715. [GAR]

GRAHAM, LENNARD, a Scottish soldier in the company of Colonel Brock, and his wife Christina Bruce, living in Captain Ymen's alley, testament, 14 December 1635. [GAR.ONA.195.231.442]

GRAHAM, MARY, widow of David Hadden a corporal in Colonel Colyear's Regiment in Flanders, a petition, 1698. [NRS.GD220.6.1749]

GRANT, GREGORY, from Burnside, Scotland, and Sarah Lombe from Norwich, England, were married in the Scots Kirk in Rotterdam on 1 May 1756. [GAR]

GRANT, JOHN, from Edinburgh, bound from Amsterdam to America, 20 April 1784. [GAA.NA.15621/251]

GRANT, WILLIAM, from Edinburgh, was admitted as a citizen of Rotterdam in 1735. [GAR]; a merchant in Rotterdam, 1747. [NRS.AC10.327]

GRANT, WILLIAM, from Scotland, was admitted as a citizen of Rotterdam in 1774. [GAR]

GRAY, ANDREW, from Aberdeen, and Jean Yeats from Aberdeen, were married in the Scots Kirk in Rotterdam on 4 July 1767. [GAR]

GRAY, DAVID, from Pittenweem, Fife, was admitted as a citizen of Rotterdam in 1720. [GAR]

GRAY, JACK, from Dundee, and Bessie Jones from Dysart, Fife, were married in Rotterdam on 25 August 1619. [GAR]

GRAY, JOHN, a Scot, was married in Bergen op Zoom, Brabant, on 28 April 1719. [WBA]

GRAY, ROBERT, a young man from Peterhead, Aberdeenshire, a seaman under Captain Jacob Cleydijck, testament, 3 December 1658, refers to William Robertson, a seafarer, and his wife Lijsbet Jansdochter, living in Ariensen Alley on the Schiedam dyke. [GAR.ONA.217.53.199]

GRAY, DAVID, from Pittenweem, Fife, was admitted as a citizen of Rotterdam on 27 September 1720. [GAR]

GRAY, THOMAS, from Bo'ness, West Lothian, was admitted as a citizen of Rotterdam in 1745. [GAR]

GRAY, WILLIAM, from Queensferry, West Lothian, and Barbara George, were married in the Scots Kirk in Rotterdam on 16 July 1721. [GAR]

GREGORIE, DAVID, took an Oath of Allegiance to King George II, in Veere, Zealand, in 1736; In 1738 he was appointed as an executor of the will of Reverend Charles Jervay minister of the Scots Kirk in Rotterdam. He was appointed as an Official Factor of the Scots Staple at Veere in 1740. [NRS.RH11.2.1]

GREGORIE, GEORGE, a Scottish factor in Veere, Zealand, took an Oath of Allegiance to King George II, in Veere, in 1728. [NRS.RH11.2.1]

GREGORIE, JOHN, a merchant in Veere, Zealand, a deed, 1702. [NRS.RD4.90.394]

GREGORIE, GEORGE, in Veere, Holland, referred to in the will of Robert Elliot in Demerara, 1779. [NRS.RD4.235.748]

GREGOIE, KENNETH, from Chanonry, Easter Ross, and Margaret Strang widow of John Wilson, were married in the Scots Kirk in Rotterdam on 29 September 1723. [GAR]

GREGORIE, WILLIAM, a skipper from Dundee and an assessor at the Scots Court in Veere, Zealand, in 1729. [NRS.RH11.2.1]

GRIERSON, JOHN, from Nithsdale, Dumfries-shire, was admitted as a citizen of Rotterdam on 9 October 1715. [GAR]

GRIERSON, ROBERT, collector of the impost in Veere, Zealand, 1635. [SHS.6/3]

GRIEVE, ANDREW WILLIAMSON, from Aberdeen, and Jannetien Beer in Rotterdam, were married in Rotterdam on 4 March 1677. [GAR]

GRIEVE, JOHN, a Scotsman from 'Dromlaenderie', [Drumlanrig, Dumfries-shire?] under Captain Leendert

Adryaenszoon Haechswant, testament, 2 May 1630, referred to William Johnston another Scot. [GAR.ONA.128/308/808]

GRIEVE, WILLIAM, in Kirkcaldy, Fife, testament, 13 March 1693, refers to Captain Johan van Convent, and to Marjory Livingstone, daughter of George Livingstone, verger of the Scots Kirk in Rotterdam. [GAR.ONA.123.73.166]

GUNN, JOHN, a Scottish seaman under Captain Bonaert, testament, 1 April 1633, refers to his wife Janneken Michelsdochter. [GAR.ONA.193/16/24]

GUNNAR, HANS, a Dutch gunner in the service of Aberdeen, 1548. [Aberdeen Burgh Records]

HACKET, GEORGE, Conservator of the Scots Privileges at Veere Zealand, from 1555 until 1589. [SSV.173]

HAIG, ANDREW, a gunner under Captain Jan Jansen of Nieuwmegen, testament, 23 March 1624, refers to Sergeant William Scott under Captain Hacket, Scotsmen. [GAR.ONA.118.53.113]

HAIGE, THOMAS, from Kilmichael in Carrick, married Isabel Haigie, in the Scots Kirk in Rotterdam on 5 May 1701. [GAR]

HAIR, GEORGE, a Scot, was married in Bergen op Zoom, Zealand, on 23 June 1636. [WBA]

HALIBURTON, JOHN, from Edinburgh, a soldier bound for the West Indies aboard the White Swan, testament, 1 December 1638, refers to Robert Hardy, a butcher, and his wife Janneken Craeck living in the Trousteech. [GAR.ONA.198.167.246]

HALKET, ALEXANDER, a Captain in the service of the States General of the Netherlands, 1699-1740. [NRAS.872.5]

HALKET, CHARLES, a Captain in the service of the States General of the Netherlands, 1708-1746. [NRAS.872.6]

HALLY, JOHN, from Perth, and Ann Mey from Rotterdam, were married in the Scots Kirk in Rotterdam 29 March 1760.[GAR]

HAMILTON, ALEXANDER, was granted a pass to travel from England to Holland on 21 September 1706. [TNA.SP44.393.91]

HAMILTON, CHRISISTOMUS, born in Ypres, Flanders, son of William Hamilton, a grant of naturalization in England, 1660. [Patent Roll, 12 Car ii.58]

HAMILTON, GEORGE, from Redhouse in Scotland, was admitted as a citizen of Rotterdam in 1720. [GAR]

HAMILTON, Sir HANS, in Utrecht, a letter, 1724. [NRS.GD24.3.299][he died in 1730]

HAMILTON, JOHN, in Bergen op Zoom, Zealand, a notarial deed, 1668. [WBA]

HAMILTON, JOHN JAMES, from Bo'ness, West Lothian, and Grietje Elzevier from Rotterdam, were married in the Scots Kirk in Rotterdam on 30 April 1679. [GAR]

HAMILTON, Major JOHN, was granted a pass to travel from England to Holland on 18 April 1706. [TNA.SP44.390.432]

HAMILTON, JOHN, from "Motsebury" in Scotland, was admitted as a citizen of Rotterdam in 1756. [GAR]

HAMILTON, ROBERT, in Leeuwarden, a letter, 1683. [NRS.CH3.269.17]

HAMILTON, WALTER, a surgeon lieutenant in Ghent, Flanders, letters, 1744. [NRAS.3339.50.2; 2522.CA14.72]

HAM, SANDER JACOBS, a shoemaker, and his wife Janneken Jans, born in Scotland, a testament, 17 June 1610. [GAR.ONA.16/12/34]

HANCOCK, FRANCISCA, relict of Arent Sonmans in Rotterdam, title to lands in East New Jersey, 1683-1685. [NRS.RH15.131]

HANCOCK, JOHN, of Wallyford, East Lothian, title to lands in East New Jersey, 1683-1685. [NRS.RH15.131]

HARCUS, ROBERT, from Orkney, a seaman under Vice Admiral Jasper Liefhebber, testament, 27 October 1632, refers to Anne Adams his landlady in Swan Alley, Rotterdam. [GAR.ONA.192.241.331]

HARDY, PETER, a Scotsman, bound for the West Indies aboard the Golden Lion, testament, 14 December 1633, refers to James Sanders a Scotsman, and to the Dutch West India Company. [GAR.ONA.321.139.340]

HARMONSON, BAUCKE, master of the Joannes van Rotterdam trading between Rotterdam and Aberdeen in 1747. [NRS.E504.1.2]

HASTY, JOHN, son of Alexander Hasty in Linlithgow, West Lothian, and Agnes Watson in Rotterdam, were married in the Scots Kirk in Rotterdam on 28 June 1725. [GAR]

HASTY, JOHN, from Bo'ness, West Lothian, was admitted as a citizen of Rotterdam in 1740. [GAR]

HAY, ALEXANDER, a Scot, was married in Bergen-op-Zoom, Brabant, on 30 December 1654. [WBA]

HAY, ALEXANDER, from Old Aberdeen, and Elizabeth Dick from Stonehaven, Kincardineshire, were married in the Scots Kirk in Rotterdam on 18 January 1703. [GAR]

HAY, DAVID, died in Surinam on 30 October 1807. [SM.70.399]

HAY, JAMES, from Buchan, Aberdeenshire, a gunner aboard the Seelandia bound for the East Indies, testament, 13 January 1648, refers to John Sibbet and his wife Lijsbet Jacobsdochter. [GAR.ONA.209.90.157]

HAY, JAMES, from Bo'ness, West Lothian, and Clara Somervliet in Rotterdam, were married in Rotterdam on 7 October 1727. [GAR]

HAY, JOHN, ["Jan Ha"] from Aberdeen, married Geertgen Gray from Scotland, in Rotterdam on 7 November 1632. [GAR]

HAY, Lord JOHN, was granted a pass to travel from England to Holland on 24 September 1706. [TNA.SP44.393.98]

HAY, ROBERT, a Scot, was married in Bergen op Zoom, Zealand, on 14 April 1626. [WBA]

HAY, WALTER, from Aberdeen, was admitted as a citizen of Rotterdam in 1741. [GAR]

HAY, WALTER, from Scotland, was admitted as a citizen of Rotterdam in 1743. [GAR]

HAY, WILLIAM, from Scotland, and Leentgen Wouters from Brabant, were married in Rotterdam on 3 March 1602. [GAR]

HAY, Lord WILLIAM, was granted a pass to travel from England to Holland on 24 September 1706. [TNA.SP44.393.98]

HAY, WILLIAM, of Drumelzier, Peebles-shire, in Rotterdam, a letter, 1709. [NRAS.2720.783]

HEINSON, JOHN, from Banff, was admitted as a citizen of Rotterdam in 1745. [GAR]

HENDERSON, ALEXANDER, in Amsterdam, a letter, 1692. [NRS.CS96.1726.6]

HENDERSON, HENRY, graduated MD from the University of Leiden, Holland, a diploma, 19 May 1653. [NRS.GD18.2033]

HENDERSON, JAMES, [Jacop Henricxone], a Scots merchant, was admitted as a burgess of Antwerpen, Flanders, in 1537. [SAA]

HENDERSON, JAMES, from Carriden, West Lothian, and Agnes Reid in Rotterdam, were married in the Scots Kirk in Rotterdam on 23 February 1734. [GAR]

HENDERSON, THOMAS, from Grangepans, West Lothian, and Janet Reid in Rotterdam, were married in the Scots Kirk in Rotterdam on 18 January 1725. [GAR]

HENDRICKS, BROER, a Dutch harpooner aboard the North Star of Dunbar whaling off Greenland in 1752. [NRS.E508.49.8]

HENDRICKSEN, WILLEM, master of the St Peter of Sardam, 1629. [NRS.AC7.2]

HENRICSON, WILLIAM, a Scots linen weaver in Bergen-op-Zoom, an inventory, 1489. [GAB.inv.3092. fo.34v]

HENRYSON, THOMAS, a Scottish workman, and Nellie Brown, his wife, living above 'The King of England' in Sant Street, a testament, 27 November 1656. [GAR.ONA.216.39.140]

HENSHIL, ['Hennipsael'], THOMAS, a Scots seaman under Captain Michael Franszoon van den Berch, testament, 9 November 1651, refers to Alexander Johnson a Scots seaman under Captain Henrick de Munnick and his wife Aertge Jans. [GAR.ONA.212.136.268]

HEPBURN, PATRICK, was granted a pass to travel from England to Holland on 21 September 1706. [TNA.SP44.393.91]

HEPBURN, WILLIAM, was granted a pass to travel from England to Holland on 4 June 1706. [TNA.SP44.393.2]

HERCULES, ALEXANDER, a Scottish gunner in the service of the Dutch East India Company, testament refers to his wife Christina Mudie in Leith, Midlothian, 14 December 1619. [GAR.ONA.37/141/305]

HERRIES, JOHN, from Dumfries, was admitted as a citizen of Rotterdam in 1745. [GAR]

HERRIES, ROBERT, from Dumfries, was admitted as a citizen of Rotterdam in 1753. [GAR]

HEWIT, JANE, widow of Gabriel Old, living in Rotterdam, appointed Captain Charles Boyd in Edinburgh as he attorney re property in Kilmarnock, Ayrshire, left to her by her late uncle Gabriel Simpson and his daughter Martha Simpson, 5 February 1723, signed by James de Bergh a notary. [NRS.GD3.963]

HINDRIKSON, HINDRIK C., master of the <u>Vriendschap</u> bound from Rotterdam to Perth, a bill of laiding, 1799. [NRS.B59.37.13.48]

HILL, ALEXANDER, from Aberdeen, and Mary Clark from Aberdeen, were married in Rotterdam on 20 February 1709. [GAR]; was admitted as a citizen of Rotterdam on 13 October 1716. [GAR]

HILL, ALEXANDER, was admitted as a citizen of Rotterdam in 1799. [GAR]

HILL, ANDREW, from St Ninians, Stirlingshire, and Maria Kerr in Rotterdam, were married in Rotterdam on 21 January 1722. [GAR]

HILL, ROBERT, from Dunmuir, and Agnes Dunmuir from Bo'ness, West Lothian, were married in the Scots Kirk in Rotterdam on 19 July 1707. [GAR]

HODGE, JOHN, ["Jan Hogs"], from Edinburgh, and Lysbeth Sanders from Scotland, were married in Rotterdam on 1 September 1647. [GAR]

HODGE, JOHN, a Scot, was married in Bergen op Zoom, Zealand, on 15 August 1710. [WBA]

HOGG, JOHN, from Dunbar, East Lothian, was admitted as a citizen of Rotterdam in 1733. [GAR]

HOGG, WILLIAM, from Veere, Zealand, and Euphan Storie in Rotterdam, were married in the Scots Kirk in Rotterdam on 8 September 1723. [GAR]

HOLLAER, CLAES, a merchant in Zierikzee, trading with Montrose, Angus, in 17... [NRS.AC10.121]

HOLMAN, WILLIAM, jr., a merchant in Vlissingen, Zealand, 1782. [NRS.CS17.1.1/153]

HOME, EDWARD, from Leddington, was admitted as a citizen of Rotterdam on 19 June 1711. [GAR]

HOME, JOHN, was appointed Conservator of the Scots Privileges at Veere, Zealand, in 1764. [SSV.260]

HOOD, ANDREW, ['Andreas Hudde'], from Dundee, a sergeant in the service of the Dutch West India Company in Brazil, 1644. [GAA.NA.1629/1095]

HOOG, WILLIAM, a merchant in Rotterdam, papers, 1753-1798. [NRS.GD215.181-183]

HOPE, JOHN, a Scottish merchant, was admitted as a burgess of Antwerpen, Flanders, in 1544. [SAA]

HOUSTON, JAMES, a merchant in Amsterdam, son of John Houston a merchant in Edinburgh, 1640. [GAA.NA.849/9]

HUME, JAMES, from Culross, Fife, a seaman under Captain Maerten Harperszoon Tromp, testament, 22 July 1632, refers to Anne Miller from Edinburgh living in Raemstaet, Rotterdam. [GAR.ONA.192/197/267]

HUNTER, ROBERT, and his wife **MARY,** were granted a pass to travel from England to Holland on 24 June 1706. [TNA.SP44.393.14]

HUNTER, ROBERT, in Veere, 1796. [NRS.CS17.1.15/80]

HUTCHEON, D., born 1773, a military surgeon in Berbice, did 7 March 1809. [SM.71.398]

INGLIS, DENNIS, guilty of forgery, banished to Flanders to serve as a soldier in the Earl of Lennox's Regiment in 1692. [NRS.GD26.7.75]

INGLIS, JOHN, in Demerara, married Helen Alves, daughter of Dr John Alves a physician in Inverness on 24 July 1798. [SM.60.575]

INNES, Sir HARRY, in Rotterdam, 1712. [NRAS.1100.1047]

INNES, JOHN, from Edinburgh, married Cryntgen Thomas from Amsterdam, in Rotterdam on 20 March 1588. [GAR].

IRVINE, DUNCAN, from Edinburgh, married Jannetje Joris from, Hulst, in Rotterdam on 30 January 1730. [GAR]

IRVINE, HUGH, in Berbice, later in Glasgow, testament,6 February 1810, Commissariot of Glasgow. [NRS.CC9.7.77/118]

IRVINE, ROBERT, a Scottish cobbler, and his wife Mary Fleck, living in an alley off Rose Street, Rotterdam, testament, 18 March 1639. [GAR.ONA.199.22.35]

IRVINE, THOMAS, a merchant in Amsterdam, a birth brief, [no date]. [NRAS.1500.761]

IRVIN, THOMAS, from the Shetland Islands, and Mary Ross in Rotterdam, were married in the Scots Kirk in Rotterdam on 20 December 1747. [GAR]

IRVINE, WILLIAM, from Bressay, Shetland Islands, and Jane Humphrey widow of John Wilson, were married in the Scots Kirk in Rotterdam on 20 April 1746. [GAR]; was admitted as a citizen of Rotterdam in 1746. [GAR]

IRVING, JAMES, from Kirkpatrick, Dumfries-shire, was admitted as a citizen of Rotterdam on 11 March 1720. [GAR]

IRWIN, JAMES, from Brock in Scotland, and Agnes Norrie in Rotterdam, were married in Rotterdam on 21 August 1721. [GAR]

JACKSON, GEORGE, was banished to Flanders in 1686 for attending conventicles. [NRS.JC39.93]

JACKSON, PETER, from Stirling, and Elsebet Ambure from Lexmond, were married in Rotterdam on 4 July 1713. [GAR]

JACKSON, PETER, clerk to Smart Tennant a merchant in Veere, Zealand, 1778. [NRS.CS16.1.173/13]

JACOBS, GOSSE, master of the Young Boer of Friezland trading between Aberdeen and Rotterdam in 1747. . [NRS.E504.1.2]

JAMIESON, or CALDERWOOD, JOHN, from Leith, Midlothian, a seaman, testament, 11 June 1639, refers to Margaret Robertson, daughter of John Robertson, a Scottish tailor. [GAR.ONA.327.164.356]

JAMIESON, JOHN, a Scot aged 15 years, bound for the East Indies aboard the Maestricht under Captain Cornelis Fredericszoon Stuijvesant, testament, 18 April 1640, refers to his uncle Willem Franszoon and aunt Jannitge Davitsdochter living in the cellar of the Five Rings on Newhaven, Rotterdam. [GAR.ONA.200.136.183]

JAMIESON, JOHN, from Bo'ness, West Lothian, married Jannetje Pieters from Rotterdam, in Rotterdam on 19 February 1692. [GAR]

JAMIESON, JOHN, from Edinburgh, and Jannetje Bogaerts from Rotterdam, were married in Rotterdam on 6 November 1696. [GAR]

JAMIESON, JOHN, from Kelso, Roxburghshire, was admitted as a citizen of Rotterdam in 1792. [GAR]

JAMESON, LAURENCE, son of Joseph Anderson in Melbie in the Shetland Islands, and Elisabeth, daughter of William Hodge in Edinburgh, were married in the Scots Kirk in Rotterdam on 3 May 1753. [GAR]

JAMIESON, WILLIAM, from Alloa, Clackmannanshire, and Jannetje Willems widow of Robert Roberts, were married in Rotterdam on 16 December 1692. [GAR]

JANCKHIER, JAN, a merchant in Rotterdam, 1782. [NRS.CS17.1.1/63]

JANSEN, SIMON, master of the <u>Brown Horse of Wodwey</u>, near Hoorn in Holland, 1628. [NRS.AC7.1]

JEMIA, ANDREW, from Bervie, Kincardineshire, and Elisabeth Michie a widow, were married in the Scots Kirk in Rotterdam on 23 May 1767. [GAR]

JERVEY, Reverend CHARLES, born 1701, minister of the Scots Kirk in Rotterdam from October 1730 until his death on 13 August 1738. On 15 August 1738 the Scots Court in Veere, Zealand, appointed Dr Alexander Anderson, David Gregorie, James Turing and Charles Stuart to act as his executors. [NRS.RH11.2.1][F.7.542][SSV.317-318]

JOHNSON, ANDREW, from Dundee, and Elisabeth Shaw from Newcastle, England, were married in the Scots Kirk in Rotterdam on 11 November 1750. [GAR]

JOHNSON, CHRISTINA, wife of Alexander Johnson a seafarer, living at the Roosant, testament, 17 September 1664, refers to her son Robert Robertson, her daughters Elizabeth and Helena Robertson. [GAR.ONA.222.67.270]

JOHNSON, DANIEL, a Scottish seaman aboard the <u>Shartogenbosch</u>, Captain Cornelis Leendertszoon, bound for the East Indies, testament, 9 December 1636, refers to Captain Sijbert Vijgh, John Wemyss, Pieter van Briel, Maertgen Lamberts, Pieter Jansz Hesainneur, Willem Bartelsz., Pieter Claesz., Jan Woutersz., and Jan Jacobs. [GAR.ONA.197.6.06]

JOHNSON, DAVID, Scotsman, midshipman aboard the ship <u>Maestricht</u>, Commander Coulster, bound for the East Indies, testament, 29 December 1636, refers to Andrew Sanderson and his wife Lijsbet Gijsbertsdochter. [GAR.ONA.197.51.51]

JOHNSON, JAMES, from Culross, Fife, and Christian daughter of Andrew Duncan in Burntisland, Fife, were married in the Scots Kirk in Rotterdam on 19 November 1704. [GAR]

JOHNSON, JOHN, from Leith, Midlothian, a tailor in Veere, Zealand, inventory, 30 May 1524. [GAV.Inv.920]

JOHNSON, JOHN, from Leith, Midlothian, and Lysbeth Pieters from Rotterdam, were married in Rotterdam on 1 January 1636. [GAR]

JOHNSON, JOHN, from Falkirk, Stirlingshire, and his wife Mary Watt, living in the New Sevenhuysen on the Schiedam dyke, testament, 2 March 1651. [GAR.ONA.211.220.406]

JOHNSON, JOHN, from Edinburgh, a seaman under Captain Pauwel van de Kerckhof, testament, 3 April 1653, refers to Jan Simonszoon, a seafarer, and his wife Grietge Davitsdochter. [GAR.ONA.214.41.134]

JOHNSON, JOHN, from Leith, Midlothian, and Barbara Jans from Delft, Holland, were married in Rotterdam on 7 February 1666.[GAR]

JOHNSON, JOHN a Scot, was married in Bergen-op-Zoom on 1 January 1681. [WBA]

JOHNSON, JOHN, from Dunbar, East Lothian, and Jannetje Jans from Rotterdam, were married in Rotterdam on 20 May 1709. [GAR].

JOHNSON, JOHN, from Leith, Midlothian, was admitted as a citizen of Rotterdam on 13 September 1714. [GAR]

JOHNSON, JOHN, from Linlithgow, West Lothian, was admitted as a citizen of Rotterdam on 2 March 1716. [GAR]

JOHNSON, JOHN, from Falkirk, Stirlingshire, and Maria Van Der Berg from Rotterdam, were married in Rotterdam on 2 November 1734. [GAR]

JOHNSON, PETER, from Aberdeen, and Tanneken Jans from Antwerp, were married in Rotterdam on 21 February 1588. [GAR]

JOHNSON, THOMAS, a linen weaver in Bergen-op-Zoom, inventory, 1501. [GAB.Inv.3092.62v]

JOHNSON, THOMAS, 'schieman' under Captain Rut Maximilianszoon aboard the <u>Wassener</u>, testament, 3 April 1666, refers to his youngest brother Charles Johnson a shoemaker living in Pepper Street, Rotterdam, his oldest brother James Johnson a seafarer, his mother Janet Thomson in Edinburgh. [GAR.ONA.224.10.34]

JOHNSON, THOMAS, from Edinburgh, and Grietge Ritt from Rotterdam, were married in Rotterdam on 4 July 1724. [GAR], was admitted as a citizen of Rotterdam in 1722. [GAR]

JOHNSON, WILLIAM, from Edinburgh, and Christina Stewart widow of Daniel Cammer, were married in Rotterdam on 29 March 1630. [GAR]

JOHNSON, WILLIAM, from Dysart, Fife, seaman under Captain Henrick Jans de Jonge Munnick, testament, 5 November 1632, refers to his mother Grietge Bruyns living in Leiden, Holland. [GAR.ONA.192/249/341]

JOHNSON, WILLIAM, [Willem Janse], from Bo'ness, West Lothian, was admitted as a citizen of Rotterdam in 1745. [GAR]

JOHNSTON, ARCHIBALD, a surgeon, son of John Johnston a writer in Bathgate, West Lothian, died in Berbice in December 1806. [SM.69.638]

JOHNSTON, JAMES, from Glasgow, and Mary Laurenc, were married in the Scots Kirk in Rotterdam on 18 January 1747. [GAR]

JOHNSTONE, JAMES, a merchant in Vlissingen, Zealand, later in Edinburgh, husband of Julia Macintosh in Vlissingen, were married on 5 February 1758 and divorced in 1785, her procurator was Adriaan van Doorn Geene a notary public in Vlissingen. [NRS.CC8.6.739]

JOHNSTON, JAMES, sometime a merchant in Ostend, Flanders, later in Edinburgh, 1785. [NRS.CS17.1.1.4/24]

JOHNSTON, JOHN, in Amsterdam, a letter, 1698. [NRAS.2171.1449]

JOHNSTON, JOHN, a Scot, was married in Bergen op Zoom, Zealand, on 17 January 1714. [WBA]

JOHNSTONE, ROBERT, Captain of Colonel Marjorybank's Regiment in Holland, heir to his brother Captain James Johnstone of Wamphrey, Dumfries-shire, who died 14 December 1745, in 1746. [NRS.S/H]

JOP, PITER, a barber-surgeon and apothecary, only son of Pitir Jop a burgess, was admitted as a guilds-brother of Aberdeen on 15 April 1663. [ABR]

JURRANS, FOLCART, a Dutch harpooner aboard the North Star of Dunbar whaling off Greenland in 1752. [NRS.E508.51.8]

KAE, NEILL, a Scottish resident of Veere, Zealand, was appointed as master of the Congerie house of Veere in 1613. [SSN.147]

KEIR, JOHN, a Scottish soldier under Captain Moy Lambrecht, testament refers to Willem Adolffszoon a tailor, 19 December 1622. [GAR.ONA.103/212/356]

KEIR, Captain NICOLAS, indweller in Den Haag, deed, 1 December 1658. [NRS.RH15.75.2]

KEIR, PATRICK, from Culross, Fife, husband of Magdalen Houston, in Amsterdam 1640, brother-in-law of James Houston a merchant in Amsterdam and son-in-law of John Houston a merchant in Edinburgh. [GAA.NA.849/9]

KEIRIE, CHARLES, in Rotterdam, letters, 1707. [NRS.GD124.15.702]

KEITH, ELIZABETH, from Scalloway in the Shetland Islands, married Roelef Berry, from Philadelphia, in the Scots Kirk in Rotterdam on 6 February 1765. [GAR]

KEITH, JAMES, from Thurso, Caithness, and Bessy, daughter of John Innis and widow of John Reid, were married in the Scots Kirk in Rotterdam on 1 April 1706. [GAR]

KEITH, PATRICK, eldest son of Reverend Keith in Golspie, Sutherland, died in Berbice on 10 August 1805. [SM.68.78]

KELTY, ALEXANDER, from Leith, Midlothian, was admitted as a citizen of Rotterdam in 1742. [GAR]

KEMPT, NICOLAS, Captain of the Tyning of Veere, was admitted as a burgess of Aberdeen on 15 July 1623. [ABR]

KENNEDY, Sir ANDREW, of Clowburn, an elder of the Scots Church in Rotterdam, 1691-1694; Conservator of the Scots Privileges of the Dutch Netherlands, a letter, 1691; a deed, 1702. He died in 1717. [NRS.GD36.13.73; RD3.98.531; RH11.2.1] [SSV.252]

KENNEDY, ANDREW, son of Sir Andrew Kennedy, a merchant and Conservator of the Scots Privileges at Veere, Zealand, in 1718. [GAV]

KENNEDY, DUNCAN, an Ensign of Collier's Regiment in Holland, heir to his wife Janet Robertson, daughter of Alexander Robertson of Struan, Perthshire, in 1740. [NRS.S/H]

KENNEDY, HAMILTON, a student in Leiden, Holland, a certificate, 1724. [NRS.GD80.119]

KENNEDY, JAMES, in Brussels, pp. 1677-1678. [NRS.GD149.332]

KENNEDY, Sir JAMES, Conservator of the Scots Privileges of the Dutch Netherlands, a letter, 1684, [CWF.MS46.02]; a deed, 1715. [NRS.RD4.116.379]

KENNEDY, THOMAS, a surgeon in the service of the States General of the Netherlands, died by 1678, son of John Kennedy of Kermucks, Orkney. [NRS.GD1.460.13]

KENNEDY, THOMAS, graduated from Leiden University, Holland, on 7 March 1681. [UL]

KENNOWAY, CHARLES, from Cramond, Midlothian, was admitted as a citizen of Rotterdam in 1745. [GAR]

KEY, JOHN, from Arbroath, Angus, was admitted as a citizen of Rotterdam in 1761. [GAR]

KEY, WILLIAM, from Greenock, Renfrewshire, and Jane Willemse, were married in the Scots Kirk in Rotterdam on 22 April 1743. [GAR]

KIDD, JAMES, a merchant in Amsterdam, 1641. [GAA.NA.849/19]

KINCAID, GEORGE, a burgess of Veere, Zealand, a sasine, 1570, [NRS.RH6.2203; RH6.2217]; a Scottish merchant in Veere, raised a Scottish company of soldiers to aid the Dutch in their struggle with the Spanish in 1573. [SSV.178]

KINCAID, JAMES, from Edinburgh, and Grietge Jans a widow from F, Zealand, were married in Rotterdam on 1 May 1585. [GAR]

KINCAID, ROBERT, factor to ...De Voes in Rotterdam, 1704. [NRS.AC8.16]

KINNEGHEE, JOHN, from Edinburgh, a soldier under Captain Prop, and Anneken Jans from Vlissingen, Zealand, were married in Rotterdam on 1 May 1588. [GAR]

KINNIMONT, ALEXANDER, from Edinburgh, was married in Bergen op Zoom, Zealand, on 20 August 1718. [WBA]

KINTOIR, ROBERT, from the Shetland Islands, a gunner aboard the <u>New Rotterdam</u> bound for the East Indies, testament, 25 March 1641, refers to his father James Kintoir in Scalloway, Shetland Islands. [GAR.ONA.201.241.327]

KIRK, JAMES, from Scotland, was admitted as a citizen of Rotterdam in 1799. [GAR]

KIRKPATRICK, J., in Utrecht, a letter, 1647. [NRS.GD402.2.44]

KNEIPER, JAN, master of the <u>Concordia van Rotterdam</u> trading between Rotterdam and Aberdeen in 1748. . [NRS.E504.1.2]

KNIGHT, ALEXANDER, from Aberdeen, was admitted as a citizen of Rotterdam in 1776. [GAR]

KNOX, JOHN, a Scot, was married in Bergen-op-Zoom on 14 September 1685. [WBA]

KNOX, JOHN, from 'Canan in Scotland' [?], was admitted as a citizen of Rotterdam in 1740. [GAR]

KROON, PETER, master of the Fish of Rotterdam trading between Rotterdam and Aberdeen in 1749. [NRS.E504.1.3]

"LACHLY" JOHN, from Edinburgh, and Margaret Forbes from Edinburgh, were married in Rotterdam on 27 June 1694. [GAR]

LAING, DAVID, a seaman before the Scots Court in Veere, Zealand, in 1728. [NRS.RH11.2.1]

LAING, WILLIAM, in Glasgow, master of the brigantine Susanna trading with St Eustatius, 1753-1754. [NRS.CS96.646]

LAMB, ALEXANDER, a Scot, was married in Bergen—op-Zoom, Zealand, on 26 August 1733. [WBA]

LAMB, ROBERT, from Leith, Midlothian, and Euphan Brown from Kirkcaldy, Fife, were married in the Scots Kirk in Rotterdam on 11 July 1736. [GAR]

LAMOND, DUNCAN, a Scot, was married in Bergen op Zoom, Zealand, on 29 February 1708. [WBA]

LANDERTSEANKER, JAN, master of the Lamachlild of Zierikseek in Montrose, Angus, 17... [NRS.AC10.121]

LARGS, ALEXANDER, from Linlithgow, West Lothian, and Grisel Legat from Rotterdam, were married in the Scots Kirk in Rotterdam on 15 December 1708. [GAR]

LAURENSON, GEORGE, from Scotland, and Janneken Sanders widow of Adam Jacobsen a carpenter, were married in Rotterdam on 21 December 1636. [GAR]

LAURIE, JAMES, eldest son of John Laurie in Glasgow, died in Curacao on 10 July 1809. [SM.70.799]

LAWRENSON, JAMES, from the Shetland Islands, and Margaret Kerr from Rotterdam, were married in the Scots Kirk in Rotterdam on 1 November 1717. [GAR]

LAURENSON, WILLIAM, from Lerwick in the Shetland Islands, and Mary Lawson from Rotterdam, were married in the Scots Kirk in Rotterdam on 24 December 1746. [GAR]

LAURIE, ROBERT, from Falkirk, Stirlingshire, and Margaret Black from Scotland, were married in the Scots Kirk in Rotterdam in August 1712. [GAR]

LAUTET, DUNCAN, from Cavenston in Orkney, married Janet Readie from Fife, were married in the Scots Kirk in Rotterdam on 26 May 1706. [GAR]

LAW, JOHN, son of David Law in Alloa, Stirlingshire, and Helen Wilson widow of Walter Kirk, were married in the Scots Kirk in Rotterdam on 10 April 1727. [GAR]

LAWSON, ISAAC, in Leiden, Holland, a letter, 1734. [NRS.GD18.5094]

LAWSON, JAMES, from Bo'ness, West Lothian, and Helen Stewart from Sunderland, England, were married in the Scots Kirk in Rotterdam on 1 March 1753. [GAR]

LAWSON, WILLIAM, from Ferryburn, and Margaret Murray from Bo'ness, West Lothian, were married in the Scots Kirk in Rotterdam on 19 June 1709. [GAR]

LEARMONTH, WILLIAM, in Leiden, Holland, a letter, 1694. [NRS.GD18.5195]

LEATHES, WILLIAM, in Brussels, letters, 1716-1722. [NRS.GD158.1534]

LEES, WILLIAM, from Dundee, a gunner's mate under the King of Portugal, Don Juan de Vierde, by skipper Stoffel Jacobs, testament, 24 June 1641, refers to James Cockburn and his wife Janet Hamilton living on the Schiedam dyke. [GAR.ONA.202.142.185]

LEES, WILLIAM, a seaman aboard the .... of Enckhuysen, Captain Cool, testament, 25 January 1642, refers to his wife Elisabeth Clerk now in Scotland, John Walker a Scot and Elisabeth Barton wife of his brother in Zealand. [GAR.ONA.355.65.162]

LENNOX, or JONES, DAVID, a Scotsman, and his wife Catherine Davidson or Mushet, a testament, 15 September 1629. [GAR.ONA.107.136.187]

LENNOX, JOHN, from Dunblane, Stirlingshire, was admitted as a citizen of Rotterdam in 1727. [GAR]

LESH, HANS, a Tavernier, was admitted as a burgess of Antwerpen, Flanders, in 1589. [SAA]

LESLIE, DAVID, Lord Balgonie, matriculated at Gronigen University, Friesland, in 1740, [NRS.GD26.11.81] a student at Groningen University, 1749-1742. [NRS.26.13.613-615] , was admitted as a citizen of Rotterdam in 1738. [GAR]

LESLIE, GEORGE, from St Monance, Fife, a steward under Captain Willem Bouwerszoon Keertdekoe, testament, 24 May 1634, refers to William Johnston and his wife Janet Watson living in Jan Joris Alley, Rotterdam. [GAR.ONA.194.169.260]

LIKELY, JAMES, from Aberdeen, minister of the Scots kirk in Veere, Zealand, from 1790 until 1799. [SSV.329]

LIND, GEORGE, Provost of Edinburgh, was appointed as Conservator of the Scots Privileges at Veere, Zealand, in 1762 but resigned a year later. [SSV.259]

LINDSAY, GEORGE, in Leiden, Holland, a letter, 1688. [NRS.RH15.106.650]

LINDSAY, Captain JOHN, witnessed a deed in Amsterdam in 1629. [NRS.GD84.2.177]

LINGISTER, [?], THOMAS, from Scotland, was admitted as a citizen of Rotterdam in 1744. [GAR]

LIVINGSTONE, ALEXANDER, from Aberdeen, was admitted as a citizen of Rotterdam in 1739. [GAR]

LIVINGSTONE, Sir JAMES, of Brighose, Colonel of a regiment in the service of the United Provinces, a deed, 1626. [NRS.GD86.480/484]

LIVINGSTONE, JOHN, son of John Livingstone a coal-grieve in Penston, an apprentice of Walter Orrock a cordiner burgess of Edinburgh, absconded and enlisted in Drumlanrig's regiment bound for Holland, 1748. [NRS.AC10.338]

LIVINGSTONE, ROBERT, born 13 December 1654, son of Reverend John Livingstone in Ancrum, Roxburghshire. The family fled to Rotterdam in 1663. Robert emigrated to Albany, New York, in 1674 where he was a merchant and colonial administrator, he died in 1728. [NRS.GD1.479/880] [SPAWI, 1687/1699][SCS]

LLOYD, ["LUID"], ADAM, from Old Meldrum, Aberdeenshire, was admitted as a citizen of Rotterdam on 29 April 1709. [GAR]

LOCKHART, GEORGE, of Carnwath, Lanarkshire, in Brussels, a letter, 1727. [NRS.GD3.5.965]

LOCKHART, JOHN, of Lee, Lanarkshire, in Leiden, Holland, a letter, 1727. [NRAS.332.C3.1227]

LOGAN, JAMES, a Scot, was married in Bergen op Zoom, Brabant, on 14 May 1719. [WBA]

LOLLING, GERRET SAMUEL, a Dutch harpooner aboard the Argyll of Campbelltown whaling off the coast of Greenland in 1751. [NRS.E508.48.8]

LOMBE, THOMAS, a merchant in Rotterdam, an inventory, 1767. [NRS.CS228.A3.36]

LORENTS, BOOIJ, a Dutch harpooner aboard the City of Aberdeen of Aberdeen whaling off Greenland in 1754. [NRS.E508.51.8]

LOVE, JAMES, from Glasgow, a soldier on board the Seelandia, master Corneilis Leenertszoon Blau, bound for the East Indies, testament, 8 January 1648, refers to a Scotsman 'Aert' Johnson and his wife Janneken Willemsdochter. [GAR.ONA.209.83.147]

LOW, ALEXANDER, from Inverness, was admitted as a citizen of Rotterdam in 1769. [GAR]

LOWE, ARTHUR, from Bo'ness, West Lothian, was admitted as a citizen of Rotterdam on 9 November 1716. [GAR]

LOW, WILLIAM, a merchant, died in Berbice on 8 June 1802. [EA.4054.02][GkA.88]

LYALL, JOHN, a seaman under Captain Jan van Es the younger, a deed, 9 June 1650, refers to Peter Pate in Culross, Fife. [GAR.ONA.211.651.130]

LYON, JOHN, Scotsman, cobbler, testament, 8 December 1637, refers to Andrew Thomson and his wife Janet Roberts, her sister Margaret Roberts, and Janet Henderson in New Haven, Rotterdam. [GAR.ONA.129.274.813]

LIVINGSTON, ALEXANDER, a servant, was granted a pass to travel from England to Holland on 4 July 1706. [TNA.SP44.393.23]

LOCKART, MARY, was granted a pass to travel from England to Holland on 25 June 1706. [TNA.SP44.393.15]

LOGAN, ROBERT, a young man from Airth, Stirlingshire, a seaman under Captain Corstiaen Eldertszoon, testament, 9 May 1659, refers to his brother James Logan living in Airth, and James Falconer the youngest child of Richard Falconer living in Jan Slijpen Alley on the Schiedam dyke. [GAR.ONA.217.92.325]

LOW, DAVID, a Scotsman, serving under Captain Jan Tijsz, testament, 18 May 1626, refers to William Johnston a Scotsman. [GAR.ONA.128/90/243]

LUMSDALE, JOHN, a skipper from Aberdeen, before the Scots Court at Veere, Zealand, in 1728; master of the Unity of Aberdeen before the Scots Court in Veere in 1739. [NRS.RH11.2.1]

LUMSDEN, JAMES, in Ostend, Flanders, a letter, 1794. [NRAS.771.266]

LYON, CHARLES, a Scot, was married in Bergen op Zoom, Brabant, on 30 June 1734. [WBA]

MACADAM, WILLIAM, from Straton, and Isobel Clunis from the Shetland Islands, were married in the Scots Kirk in Rotterdam on 13 November 1745. [GAR]

MCALISTAIR, JOHN, from Bo'ness, West Lothian, and Isobel Smith from London, were married in the Scots Kirk in Rotterdam on 5 May 1734. [GAR]

MCAULAY, ARCHIBALD, Lord Conservator of the Privileges of the Scots Nation in the Netherlands, 1719. [NRS.RH11.2.1][he died in 1760]

MACCALLA, DANIEL, son of George MacCalla in Kilmartin, Argyll, married Margaret Hunter, widow of Charles McLean, in the Scots Kirk in Rotterdam on 9 August 1736. [GAR]

MACCARTNEY, ..., in Ostend, Flanders, a letter, 1712. [NRAS.332.M3.11]

MCCASKILL, KENNETH, a surgeon, died on the Hague Plantation, Essequibo, on 11 September 1818. [EA.5749.79]

MCCELTER, DUNCAN, a Scot, was married in Bergen op Zoom, Brabant, on 22 April 1626. [WBA]

MCCONNELL, DAVID, a Scot, was married in Bergen—op-Zoom, Brabant, on 7 October 1733. [WBA]

MACCURE [?], JOHN, son of Murdoch MacCure on Lewis, Outer Hebrides, and Margaret Dixon, were married in the Scots Kirk in Rotterdam on 18 January 1725. [GAR]

MACDONALD, HUGH, son of Alexander MacDonald of Paiblesgary, bound for Holland in 1691. [NRAS.3273.244]

MACDONALD, JAMES and JOHN, were granted a pass to travel from England to Holland on 28 July 1706. [TNA.SP44.393.42]

MACDONALD, JOHN, in Berbice, eldest son of Donald McDonald sometime in Jamaica, a deed, 1809. [NRS.RD2.307.259]

MCDONALD, Mrs, widow of John McDonald on the Kintyre Plantation, Berbice, married Alexander McDuff a Lieutenant of the 100th Regiment of Foot on 18 November 1824. [S.508.829]

MCDONEL, HUBERT, a Scot, was married in Bergen op Zoom, Brabant, on 5 April 1707. [WBA]

MACDOWELL, Sir WILLIAM, His Majesty's Resident in the United Provinces, a memorandum, 1650. [NRS.GD40.2.4.14]

MCEWAN, ALEXANDER, son of William McEwan in Bo'ness, West Lothian, and Jane Huy a widow, were married in the Scots Kirk in Rotterdam on 19 March 1726. [GAR]

MCFARLAN, ANDREW, from Stirling, was admitted as a citizen of Rotterdam on 18 February 1715. [GAR]

MCFARLANE, W., was granted Glasgow Plantation in Berbice in 1792. [TNA]

MACGALDRYE, JOHN, a burgess of Veere, Zealand, died in Glasgow on 19 December 1566, husband of Grizel Johnston. [ECA.MBVII.bundle 209/7628]

MCGIE, BRODIE, from Edinburgh, and Elisabeth Kent from Newcastle, England, were married in Rotterdam on 19 March 1758. [GAR]

MCGHIE, JOHN, a Captain in the service of the States of Holland, sasines, 1767-1773. [NRS.RS23.XX.II/131; XXI.25/53] ; 1782. [NRS.CS17.1.1/129]

MAKGILL, JOHN, from Edinburgh, a seaman under Captain Dirck Gerritssoon Verburch, testament, 1 July 1628, refers to Robert McKnight ['Mijnknecht'] a Scottish soldier in the company of Colonel Brock. [GAR.ONA.183.357.512]

MCGREGOR, DUNCAN, born 1788, died in Vlissingen, Zealand, 1809, son of Gregor McGregor and his wife A. McGregor. [Killichonan MI, Fortingall, Perthshire]

MACHAN, JAMES, from St Ninian's, Stirlingshire, and Susanna Johnson, were married in the Scots Kirk in Rotterdam on 13 April 1707. [GAR]

MCILVAINE, PATRICK, a Captain of the Royal Regiment of Foot, died in Flanders, probate, 1695. [PCC]

MACINTOSH, GEORGE JAMES, from Edinburgh, and Sara Jans Made from Rotterdam, were married in Rotterdam on 25 May 1711. [GAR]

MACINTOSH, HENRY, from Inverness, planter of Fairfield Plantation on the Commewine River, Surinam, by 1675, married Elizabeth le Hunt from Port Royal, Jamaica, in 1688, died in Surinam in 1690. [Calendar of State Papers, Colonial, 1675.01][Abstract of New York Wills, liber 1-2.fos.184-185][State Papers, America and the West Indies.1675.401; 1676.943][NRS.RH15.106.567/1]

MACINTOSH, JULIA, in Vlissingen, Zealand, wife of James Johnston, a merchant in Vlissingen, later in Edinburgh, were married 5 February 1758, and divorced in 1785, her procurator was Adriaan van Doorn Geene a notary public in Vlissingen. [NRS.CC8.6.739]

MCINTOSH, WILLIAM, son of Alexander McIntosh a merchant in Inverness, born 1769, died 1802, settled in Surinam. [Kilmallie MI]

MACIVER, WILLIAM, son of Donald MacIver in Nairn, and Mary Jamieson from Muirkirk, Ayrshire, were married in the Scots Kirk in Rotterdam on 21 August 1709. [GAR]

MACKAY, ALEXANDER, from Skail, Sutherland, was admitted as a citizen of Rotterdam on 30 August 1717. [GAR]

MACKAY, DANIEL, a Scot, was married in Bergen-op-Zoom, Brabant, on 12 November 1698. [WBA]

MACKAY, JOHN, from Inverness, and Janet Dalgleish from Rotterdam, were married in Rotterdam on 11 February 1720. [GAR]; was admitted as a citizen of Rotterdam on 6 February 1719 [GAR]

MACKAY, ROBERT, a soldier at Moulaine near Namur Castle, a letter, 1695. [NRS.GD112.39.171-173]

MACKAY, ROBERT, a merchant in the Netherlands, a bill of exchange, 1726. [NRS.GD24.5.220]

MACKAY, WILLIAM, from Sutherlandshire, was admitted as a citizen of Rotterdam in 1745. [GAR]

MACKEAN, DANIEL, a servant, was granted a pass to travel from England to Holland on 5 April 1706. [TNA.SP44.390.415a]

MCKELLEN, JOHN, from Edinburgh, and Jannetje Jans from Maastricht, Limburg. were married in Rotterdam on 11 November1704. [GAR]

MCKENDRICK, WILLIAM, in Rotterdam, a bill of exchange, 1702. [NRS.GD30.477]

MACKENTER, RICHARD, from Bo'ness, West Lothian, was admitted as a citizen of Rotterdam in 1743. [GAR]

MACKENZIE, ALEXANDER, from Ross in Scotland, and Pieterne van Solingen from Delft, Holland, were married in Rotterdam on 3 September 1757. [GAR]

MCKENZIE, ANDREW, from Kintyre in Argyll, was admitted as a citizen of Rotterdam in 1740. [GAR]

MACKENZIE, GEORGE, a tutor, was granted a pass to travel from England to Holland on 11 July 1706. [TNA.SP44.393.27]

MACKENZIE, JAMES, from Inverness, and Jane Hudson from Newcastle, England, were married in the Scots Kirk in Rotterdam on 9 November 1785. [GAR]

MCKENZIE, JOHN, a Scot, was married in Bergen op Zoom, Brabant, on 24 February 1734. [WBA]

MCKENZIE, JOHN, from Gairloch, Wester Ross, was admitted as a citizen of Rotterdam in 1762. [GAR]

MACKENZIE, LACHLAN, from Cromarty, and Mary Arbottel from Sunderland, England, were married in the Scots Kirk in Rotterdam on 22 April 1769. [GAR]

MACKENZIE, LENNARD, from Scotland, was admitted as a citizen of Rotterdam in 1780. [GAR]

MACKENZIE, MURDOCH, from Inverness, was admitted as a citizen of Rotterdam on 29 February 1716. [GAR]

MACKISON, JOHN, a Scot, was married in Bergen-op-Zoom, Brabant, on 13 June 1759. [WBA]

MACKUM, WALTER, a midshipman from Edinburgh, recruited for service in the Dutch West Indies, 17 March 1640. [GAA.NA926/97]

MCLEA, WILLIAM, [Willem Mocklew], from Fraserburgh, Aberdeenshire, was admitted as a citizen of Rotterdam in 1740. [GAR]

MCLEAN, ALLAN, from Mull, Inverness-shire, married Christian Morgan from Dunfermline, Fife, in the Scots Kirk in Rotterdam on 16 January 1709. [GAR]

MCLEOD, ANGUS, a Captain in the Service of the States General of the United Netherlands, a commission, 1702-1710. [NRS.GD1.1062]

MACLEAN, CHARLES, from Montrose, Angus, was admitted as a citizen of Rotterdam in 1735. [GAR]

MCLEOD, JOHN, a Scot, was married in Bergen op Zoom, Brabant, on 26 May 1719. [WBA]

MACLEROY, STEPHEN, a journeyman saddler, was granted a pass to travel from England to Holland on 28 October 1705. [TNA.SP44.391.183]

MACMASTER, WILLIAM, son of Patrick MacMaster in Steenra [?], and Rebecca Paterson, were married in the Scots Kirk in Rotterdam on 2 March 1707. [GAR]

MACNAB, DUNCAN, from Perth, was admitted as a citizen of Rotterdam in 1767. [GAR]

MACPHERSON, ALEXANDER, from Inverness-shire, and Janet Grant widow of James Mitchell, were married in the Scots Kirk in Rotterdam on 17 March 1762. [GAR]

MACPHERSON, GEORGE, from Aberdeenshire, and Helena Kings from Maastricht, Limburg, were married in the Scots Kirk in Rotterdam on 7 June 1776. [GAR]

MACPHERSON, NEIL, from Inverness, and Janet Fordue from London, were married in Rotterdam on 20 June 1706. [GAR]

MACPHERSON, WILLIAM, son of Allan MacPherson and his wife Elizabeth in Blairgowrie, Perthshire, a planter in Berbice from 1806. [NRS.NRAS.bundle 8.10]

MACRAILT [?], JOHN, son of John MacRailt in Colborst, Inverness-shire, and Lucy Lightfoot from Durham, England, were married in the Scots Kirk in Rotterdam on 30 July 1773. [GAR]

MCRAVIE, ARCHIBALD, from Argyll, and Mary Golden from Sunderland, England, were married in the Scots Kirk in Rotterdam on 5 November 1757. [GAR]

MAINE, JAMES, a Scotsman living in Aberdour, Fife, a sailor, testament, 23 February 1651, refers to his Scottish wife Elizabeth Bryson living in New Haven, Rotterdam. [GAR.ONA.211.214.395]

MAIN, ROBERT, an elder of the Scots Church in Rotterdam, 1645-1652. [GAR]

MAIN, WILLIAM, from Edinburgh, was admitted as a citizen of Rotterdam in 1734. [GAR]

MALLOCH, ALEXANDER, from Edinburgh, and Lysbeth Barders, from Edinburgh, were married in Rotterdam on 19 September 1638. [GAR]

MALLOCH, GEORGE, was granted a pass to travel from England to Holland on 21 May 1706. [TNA.SP44.390.456]

MANDERS, ROBERT, from Dunbarton, bound for the West Indies under skipper Arien Claesz., testament, 16 December 1623, refers to his sister Margaret Anderson in Scotland and to Maycken Pietersdochter living in New Haven, Rotterdam, daughter of Captain Pieter Corsten Hort. [GAR.ONA.104/125/191]

MANSON, JAMES, from Thurso, Caithness, was admitted as a citizen of Rotterdam in 1754. [GAR]

MANSON, WILLIAM, from Caithness, was admitted as a citizen of Rotterdam in 1740. [GAR]; a merchant in Rotterdam, deceased, 1798. [NRS.CS97.111.87]

MAR, DAVID, a merchant from Aberdeen, an assessor of the Scots Court in Veere, Zealand, 1728. [NRS.RH1.2.1]

MARSHALL, ROBERT, a Scot, was married in Bergen-op-Zoom, Brabant, on 9 October 1654. [WBA]

MARTIN, ALEXANDER, from Scotland, was admitted as a citizen of Rotterdam in 1770. [GAR]

MARTIN, HELEN, from Aberdeen, was admitted as a citizen of Rotterdam in 1758. [GAR]

MARTIN, THOMAS, an elder of the Scots Church in Rotterdam, 1657-1659. [GAR]

MARTIN, WILLIAM, a Scot, was married in Bergen-op-Zoom, Brabant, on 17 February 1658. [WBA]

MASON, DAVID, from the Shetland Islands, an assessor of the Scots Court in Veere, Zealand, in 1739. [NRS.RH11.2.1]

MASTERTON, WLLIAM, from Galloway, was admitted as a citizen of Rotterdam on 24 September 1711. [GAR]

MATHESON, ALEXANDER GORDON, the youngest son of Colin Matheson of Bennetsfield, died in Berbice on 13 October 1820. [BM.8.482]

MATHESON, CHARLES, a Scot, was married in Bergen-op-Zoom, Brabant, on 28 October 1733. [WBA]

MATHESON, HENRY, from Dundee, a seaman aboard the Seecalf, Captain Jan Janszoon van de Kerckhof, testament, 23 August 1631, refers to Aeltge Cammen living in Schilders lane, Rotterdam. [GAR.ONA.191.243.320]

MATTHEWS, DAVID, from Edinburgh, and Janneke Robberts, were married in Rotterdam on 15 September 1630. [GAR]

MATTHEWS, JOHN, from Dundee, a seaman under Captain Jan van Nes, testament, 21 March 1641, refers to his brother Henry Matthews and John Nicolls son of his sister. [GAR.ONA.201.236.320]

MATHEWS, WILLIAM, ['Willem Mattis'], born 1614 in Aberdeen, a soldier in the service of the Dutch West India Company bound for Curacao aboard the Hope of Vlissingen in 1644. [GAA.NA.926/270]

MAULE, HARRY, of Kelly, a Jacobite refugee in Leiden, Holland, 1716. [NRS.GD1.616.36]; letters to his wife in Edinburgh, 1718-1719. [NRS.GD45.14.376]

MAULE, JOHN, son of Charles Maule in Leith, Midlothian, a merchant in Demerara, died 17 October 1798. [AJ.2664]

MAWER, ARCHIBALD, son of Patrick Mawer in Aberdeen, and Christian Hutcheson from Rotterdam, were married in the Scots Kirk in Rotterdam on 9 January 1727. [GAR]

MAXWELL, JOHN THOMSON, a trumpeter and a young man from Montrose, Angus, testament, 8 January 1633, refers to his wife Janet Maxwell, and to John Gillis a corporal in the company of Colonel Brock. [GAR.ONA.129.3.19]

MAXWELL, ROBERT, bound for Holland aboard the Helen of Leith, 1668. [NRS.RH15.75.9]

MEIKLE, JAMES, a millwright in Holland, 1710. [NRAS.3206]

MEIKLE, JAMES, from Bo'ness, West Lothian, was admitted as a citizen of Rotterdam in 1743. [GAR]

MEIKLEJOHN, ALEXANDER, from Carriden, West Lothian, and Anna Van Der Waart from Rotterdam, were married in Rotterdam on 30 May 1741. [GAR]

MELVILLE, ALEXANDER, from Carriden, West Lothian, and Catherine Johnston from Ireland, were married in the Scots Kirk in Rotterdam on 24 October 1708. [GAR]

MELVILLE, D., a merchant in Berbice, married Sarah, daughter of John Polson, in Old Aberdeen on 31 January 1828. [S.846.114]

MELVILLE, JOHN, in Utrecht, a letter, 1718. [NRS.GD45.31.32]

MENZIES, JOHN, born 1608, from Dundee, bound from Amsterdam to Brazil aboard the Endracht in 1644. [GAA.ONA.1289/138]

MENZIES, JOHN, a Scotsman, bound for Portugal in the service of the West India Company of Middelburg, Zealand, testament, 3 May 1649, refers to Margaret Williamsdochter. [GAR.ONA.209.247.441]

MENZIES, ["MANIUS"?], PHILIP, from Glasgow, was admitted as a citizen of Rotterdam in 1739. [GAR]

MERCER, WILLIAM, of Aldie, a Captain in the service of the States General of Holland, 1768-1770, papers. [died 1790] [NRAS.3698]

MEUG, ANDREW, son of George Meug in Ethie, Angus, and Janet Guthrie, were married in the Scots Kirk in Rotterdam on 23 November 1702. [GAR]

MIDDLETON, JANET, daughter of Robert Middleton a shearer in Edinburgh, wife of Thomas Frissell residing on the dyke near the White Lion brewery, testament, 26 March 1625, refers to Peter Muir, a Scot, and her son David Frissell. [GAR.ONA.156.34.72]

MIKKELL, JAMES, son of James Mikkell in Ecclesfechan, Dumfries-shire, and Willemynte Jans daughter of Jan Dikse in Rotterdam, were married in the Scots Kirk in Rotterdam on 19 March 1740. [GAR]

MILL, JOHN, son of William Mill in Cranston, Midlothian, and Margaret Gilles from Bo'ness, West Lothian, were married in the Scots Kirk in Rotterdam on 9 November 1712. [GAR]

MILL, WILLIAM, born in Scotland, and his wife Aeltgen Andries, in Hospital Lane, Rotterdam, a testament, 12 April 1619. [GAR.37/78/174]

MILLER, EDWARD, from Edinburgh, a widower under Captain Laurence Scott, and Janneken Weddel from Edinburgh, were married in Rotterdam on 17 August 1587. [GAR]

MILLER, JAMES, from Kinell, married Agnes Adam, in the Scots Kirk in Rotterdam on 8 December 1706. [GAR]

MILLER, JAMES, from Kippen, Stirlingshire, and Helen Jamieson, were married in the Scots Kirk in Rotterdam on 15 October 1755. [GAR]

MILLER, ROBERT, from Edinburgh, and Anna Catherina Spronk, were married in Rotterdam on 7 November 1756. [GAR]; was admitted as a citizen of Rotterdam in 1757. [GAR]

MILLER, WILLIAM, from Ayr, and Johanna Van Dulderan from Rotterdam, were married in Rotterdam on 10 September 1713. [GAR]

MILLIGAN, JOHN, from Nithsdale, Dumfries-shire, was admitted as a citizen of Rotterdam in 1733. [GAR]

MILNE, JOHN, born in Scotland, a bosun aboard the United Netherlands, Captain Jacob Cleydijck, and his wife Neeltgen Laurens, testament, 10 June 1659. [GAR.ONA.534.161.339]

MITCHELL, DAVID, son of James Mitchell in Craigie, Dundee, and Helen Barnes widow of John Hay who died at sea in April 1702, were married in the Scots Kirk in Rotterdam on 10 December 1704. [GAR]; was admitted as a citizen of Rotterdam on 29 July 1713. [GAR]

MITCHELL, JAMES, an innkeeper on the Scotsdyke, Rotterdam, a deed, 1714. [NRS.RD4.114.819]

MITCHELL, JAMES, from Bo'ness, West Lothian, and Janet Grant, were married in the Scots Kirk in Rotterdam on 21 April 1753. [GAR]; was admitted as a citizen of Rotterdam in 1756. [GAR]

MITCHELL, JOHN, a merchant in Rotterdam, 1676. [NRS.AC7.4]

MITCHELL, ROBERT, from Bo'ness, West Lothian, and Catherine Burns from Rotterdam, were married in the Scots Kirk in Rotterdam on 30 December 1716. [GAR]; was admitted as a citizen of Rotterdam on 29 January 1720. [GAR]

MTCHELL, WILLIAM, from Aberdeen, was admitted as a citizen of Rotterdam in 1753. [GAR]

MITCHELL, Dr WILLIAM, minister of the Scots Church in Leiden, Holland, a document, 1791. [NRS.GD1.6.1193]

MITCHELHILL, PETER, from Selkirk, and Mary Baxter from Northumberland, England, were married in the Scots Kirk in Rotterdam on 22 February 1758. [GAR]

MONCREIFF, WILLIAM, reader at the Scots Kirk in Veere, Zealand, took an Oath of Allegiance to King George II, in Veere, in 1728. [NRS.RH11.2.1]

MONCREIFF, ..., was granted a pass to travel from England to Holland on 22 April 1706. [TNA.SP44.390.435]

MONRO, DAVID, from Edinburgh, was admitted as a citizen of Rotterdam on 11 December 1717. [GAR]

MONRO, WILLIAM, from Largo or Largs, and Catherine McLean, were married in Rotterdam on 25 June 1746. [GAR]

MONTGOMERIE, ..., in Breda, Brabant, a letter, 1650. [NRS.GD3.5.4.473]

MONTIER, GILBERT, a merchant from Rotterdam later in Edinburgh, 1715. [NRS.AC8.197]

MOOD, WILLIAM, and Margaret Hamilton, both from the Shetland Islands, were married in the Scots Kirk in Rotterdam on 9 November 1757. [GAR]

MOORE, ELIZABETH, born 2 May 1782 in St Eustatia, Dutch West Indies, died in Edinburgh on 29 November 1870, wife of James McInroy of Lude, born 1759, died 1825. [Kilmaveanaig MI, Blair Atholl, Perthshire.]; he from Demerara, and Elizabeth Moore, from St Eustatia, were married in Broomloan on 25 December 1797. [EEC.420]

MORRAN, ALEXANDER, from Bo'ness. West Lothian, and Margaretha Thompson from England, were married in Rotterdam on 1 August 1719. [GAR]

MORRIS, ALEXANDER BRUCE, died in Berbice on 20 July 1808. [SM.70.796]

MORRIS, DAVID, a Scot, was married in Halsteren, Brabant, on 2 March 1678. [WBA]

MORRIS, JOHN, a Scots tailor in Bergen-op-Zoom, Brabant, inventory, 1513. [GAB.Inv.3092.105r]

MORRISON, GEORGE, a Scot, a soldier under Captain Wassenhoven, testament, 4 June 1623, refers to his son William Georgeson. [GAR]

MORRISON, JAMES, a merchant in Amsterdam, a letter, 1710. [NRAS.3206.5]

MORRISON, SAMUEL, from Dundee, and Margaret Ross, were married in the Scots Kirk in Rotterdam on 4 Agust 1658. [GAR]

MORRISON, THOMAS, a merchant in Leiden, Holland, sasines 1630s. [NAS.RS31.IX.190; XI.369]

MORRISON, WILLIAM, son of William Morrison in Bo'ness, West Lothian, and Janet Hendrie, were married in the Scots Kirk in Rotterdam n 14 February 1654. [GAR]

MORRISON, WILLIAM, from Bo'ness, West Lothian, was admitted as a citizen of Rotterdam on 16 February 1720. [GAR]

MORTON, JACK, a leadwinder{?}, born in Edinburgh, husband of Aeltgen Penman born in the Westport of Edinburgh, testament refers to John Thomson a Scottish clothmaker, 1 January 1618. [GAR.ONA.100/161/181]

MORTON, THOMAS, from Edinburgh, a merchant in Amsterdam, 1642, 1650. [GAA.NA.1569/413; NA.849/163]

MOSCROPE, WILLIAM, a burgess of Jedburgh, Roxburghshire, a witness in Den Haag, 1650. [NRS.GD40.6.10]

MOWAT, ANDREW, from the Shetland Islands, and Margaret McConachie, were married in the Scots Kirk in Rotterdam on 21 May 1745. [GAR]

MOWAT, RODGER, from Elgin, Morayshire, and Helen Wilson from Linlithgow, West Lothian, were married in the Scots Kirk in Rotterdam on 9 March 1712. [GAR]

MOWBRAY, THOMAS, formerly chaplain to Lord Cranston's regiment in Prussia, was appointed minister of the Scots kirk in Veere, Zealand, from 1659 until 1664. [SSV.302]

MOYES [?], ['MUS'], THOMAS, aboard a Dutch warship under Captain Merten Herpertszoon, a deed, 13 January 1628

refers to his wife in Bo'ness, West Lothian.
[GAR.ONA.106/223/305]

MUDIE, GEORGE, aged around 32, from Leith, Midlothian,
bosun aboard the Golden Star from Virginia to Amsterdam,
1664. [GAA.NA1581/495]

MUDIE, LAURENCE, from Scotland, was admitted as a
citizen of Rotterdam in 1740. [GAR]

MUDIE, WILLIAM, from Scotland, was admitted as a citizen
of Rotterdam in 1755. [GAR]

MUIR, WILLIAM, from Dundee, and Frances Butler widow
of John Taylor from Kinsale, Ireland, were married in the
Presbyterian Church in Rotterdam on 27 February 1709.
[GAR]

MUIR, WILLIAM, an elder of the Scots Church in
Rotterdam, 1643-1650. [GAR]

MUNRO, M., was granted Edinburgh Plantation in Berbice in
1792. [TNA]

MURDOCH, JOHN, from Bo'ness, West Lothian, and Janet
McCulloch from Rotterdam, were married in the Scots Kirk in
Rotterdam on 13 September 1732. [GAR]

MURDOCH, WILLIAM, from Old Meldrum, Aberdeenshire,
was admitted as a citizen of Rotterdam in 17454. [GAR]

MURDOCH and WALKER, merchants in Rotterdam, 1757.
[NRAS.3666.87]

MURRAY, AUGUSTINE, a Scotsman, bound for the West
Indies aboard the ship of Captain Verhouven, testament, 12
August 1634, refers to John Garnaert, a Scot, and his wife
Aefken Haeckere. [GAR.ONA.185.443.541]

MURRAY, DAVID, son of the laird of Rowmanna, a witness
in Den Haag, 1650. [NRS.GD40.6.10]

MURRAY, EDWARD, from Edinburgh, wss admitted as a
citizen of Rotterdam on 26 March 1710. [GAR]

MURRAY, FRANCIS, was granted a pass to travel from England to Holland on 6 April 1706. [TNA.SP44.390.416]

MURRAY, JAMES, from Dundee, and Isabella Dixon from Whitehaven, England, were married in Rotterdam on 12 June 1804. [GAR]

MURRAY, JOHN, in Ostend, Flanders, a letter, 1678. [NRAS.258.3.1.13]

MURRAY, JOHN, from Cumbernauld, Stirlingshire, and Jean Park, were married in the Scots Kirk in Rotterdam on 3 March 1706. [GAR]

MURRAY, Sir JOSEPH, Count de, a Major General of the Dutch Republic, heir to his cousin Sir Alexander Murray of Melgund in Angus. [NRS.S/H.1771]

MURRAY, KATHERINE, was granted a pass to travel from England to Holland on 6 April 1706. [TNA.SP44.390.416]

MURRAY, MICHAEL, a carpenter from Edinburgh, and Christine Davids widow of David Barber a corporal under Captain Messiner, were married in Rotterdam on 26 July 1592. [GAR]

MURRAY, THOMAS, from Leith, Midlothian, and Margaret Gardner from Scotland, were married in Rotterdam on 28 May 1595. [GAR]

MURRAY, THOMAS, from St Andrews, Fife, a seaman under Captain Joost van Colster, testament, 20 September 1651, refers to John Williams and his wife Elizabeth Hendry. [GAR.ONA.212.93.183]

MYLLAR, HANS, a Dutchman, was admitted as a burgess of Edinburgh on 23 June 1569. [EBR]

NAUGHTON, GEORGE, from Queensferry, West Lothian, and Helen Ogilvy from Rotterdam, were married in the Scots Kirk in Rotterdam on 23 December 1734. [WBA]

NAILHENCDE, JOHN, Captain of the warship Leiden of Zealand, and his son John were admitted as guilds-brothers of Aberdeen on 6 October 1659. [ABR]

NAIRN, WILLIAM, was granted a pass to travel from England to Holland on 21 September 1706. [TNA.SP44.393.91]

NAPIER, ROBERT, a Scotsman, a seaman under Captain Flips Schoneman, testament, 26 August 1641, refers to Francis Cochrane, a Scotsman, and his spouse Anneken Andriesdochter. [GAR.ONA.202.223.284]

NAUGHTON, ALEXANDER, a merchant in Rotterdam, 1724. [NRS.CS228.M2.51]

NAUGHTON, EDWARD, from Stow, Peeebles-shire, was admitted as a citizen of Rotterdam on 5 J 1710. [GAR]

NEILSON, ALEXANDER, a Scot, was married in Bergen op Zoom, Brabant, on 13 June 1717. [WBA]

NESS, JOHN, a seaman from Leith, Midlothian, testament, 21 December 1624, refers to Anna Jansdochter wife of Willem Janszoon a seaman, and Captain Jan Janszoon in Nijmegan, Gelderland. [GAR.ONA.40.106.259]

NEWTON, GEORGE, from Queensferry, West Lothian, was admitted as a citizen of Rotterdam in 1757. [GAR]

NIMMO, ROBERT, from Carriden, West Lothian, and Catherine Smith, were married in the Scots Kirk in Rotterdam on 16 June 1742. [GAR]; was admitted as a citizen of Rotterdam in 1744. [GAR]

NISBET, P., a planter in Aurora, Essequibo, in 1802. [NRS.RD3.298.262; RD3.298.256]

NOBLE, ALEXANDER, son of Arthur Noble in Bo'ness, West Lothian, and Elizabeth Noble, were married in the Scots Kirk in Rotterdam on 2 September 1779. [WBA]

NOBLE, WILLIAM, from Fraserburgh, Aberdeenshire, a young man, a gunner aboard the Lion, Captain Dirck

Gerritzoon Verbuch, testament, 21 January 1630, refers to James Cruck, a Scot and an innkeeper on the Schiedam dyke in Rotterdam, also his brothers and sisters in Scotland. [GAR.ONA.190.86.120]

NORRIE, ALEXANDER, a Scot, was married in Bergen-op-Zoom, Brabant, on 3 January 1762. [WBA]

NORRIE, JAMES, a merchant in Rotterdam, 1702. [NRS.GD45.17.815]; an elder of the Scots Church in Rotterdam, 1687-1700. [GAR]

'NOTRE, HENRICK', born 1614, from St Johnstoun, [Perth], bound from Amsterdam to Brazil aboard the Endracht in 1644. [GAA.NA.1289/138]

OGILBIE, ALEXANDER, from Leith, Midlothian, and Mary Wallace from Bo'ness, West Lothian, were married in Rotterdam on 24 August 1732. [GAR]

OGILBIE, ALEXANDER, son of John Ogilbie in Dysart, Fife, and Margaret Rattray from Wemyss, Fife, were married in the Scots Kirk in Rotterdam on 13 November 1787. [GAR]

OGILVIE, ALEXANDER, from Dundee, was admitted as a citizen of Rotterdam in 1755. [GAR]

OGILVIE, JAMES, an elder of the Scots Church in Rotterdam, 1652-1658. [GAR]

OGILVIE, ROBERT, born in Scotland, a ropeworker's mate under Captain Vijch, testament, 25 March 1635, refers to Merten Janszoon and his wife Jannitgen Henderixdochter. [GAR.ONA.111.22.41]

OGILVIE, WALTER and REBECCA, were granted passes to travel from England to Holland on 8 November 1705. [TNA.SP44.390.330]

ORBAN, ROBERT, from the Shetland Islands, a seaman under Commander Engebrecht Peterszoon van der Zee, aboard the ship of Captain Jan Brustenszoon, testament, 2 June 1628, refers to Robert Lawson and his wife Janneken

Robbrechtsdochter in Bierhaven or the New Work.
[GAR.ONA.188/227/344]

"ORFORT", JOHN, aged around 34, from Aberdeen, bosun
aboard the <u>De Jaeger</u> bound for the New Netherlands, 1650.
[GAA.NA1575/164]

OVENS, ADAM, a Scotsman, and his wife Maritge
Dircxpietersdochter, testament, 23 January 1652.
[GAR.ONA.155.148.222]

OVEN, WILLIAM, from Dundee, and Janet Smith from
Rotterdam, were married in the Scots Kirk in Rotterdam on 28
December 1712. [GAR]

PAINTON, ROBERT, in the Netherlands, an account book,
17... [NRS.GD345.916]

PANTON, ROBERT, from Aberdeen, was admitted as a
citizen of Rotterdam on 9 February 1719. [GAR]

PARISH, JOHN, a sailor, before the Scots Court in Veere,
Zealand, in 1730. [NRS.RH11.2.1]

PATERSON, DAVID, from Edinburgh, and Barbara
Dempster, were married in the Scots Kirk in Rotterdam on 14
September 1718. [GAR]

PATTERSON, GEORGE, from Dundee, and Jean Cowie
from Bo'ness, West Lothian, were married in the Scots Kirk in
Rotterdam in 1715. [WBA]

PATERSON, GEORGE, a Scot, was married in Bergen op
Zoom, Brabant, on 23 July 1734. [WBA]

PATERSON, HECTOR, in Veere, Zealand, 1623.
[GAA.NA.387/219]

PATTERSON, JAMES, was granted a pass to travel from
England to Holland on 4 June 1706. [TNA.SP44.393.2]

PATERSON, JOHN, a law student in Leiden, Holland, a
letter, 1694. [NRS.GD406.1.1009]

PATTERSON, JOHN, son of William Paterson in Airth, Stirlingshire, and Jean Cassels from Bo'ness, West Lothian, were married in the Scots Kirk in Rotterdam on 4 August 1717. [GAR]

PATON, MATTHEW, an elder of the Scots Church in Rotterdam, 1643-1647. [GAR]

PATON, PETER, from Bo'ness, West Lothian, and Mary Wallace from Rotterdam, were married in the Scots Kirk in Rotterdam on 20 December 1749. [GAR]; was admitted as a citizen of Rotterdam in 1759. [GAR]

PEEBLES, DAVID, master of the Conciergery House in Veere, Zealand, and his wife Elizabeth Cant, 1631. [SHS.6/3]

PENNY, JOHN, from 'Carin' in Scotland, a seaman under Admiral de With, bound for Brazil, testament, 16 November 1647, refers to James Randel and his wife Janneken Pietersdochter living in Vrackesteech, Rotterdam. [GAR.ONA.209.42.84]

PETERSON, CLAUS, burgess of Amsterdam, deed, 17 March 1560. [NRS.RDIV.90]

PETERSON, CORNELIS, master of the Green Drake of Alkmaar, 1628. [NRS.AC7.1]

PEUQUE, LEONARD, Captain of the Zealand of Tarbees, was admitted as a guilds-brother of Aberdeen on 4 June 1656. [ABR]

PICKEMAN, ROBERT, from Montrose, Angus, was admitted as a citizen of Rotterdam in 1754. [GAR]

PIETERS, EGBERT, master of the Walveren van de Eniegste van Groningen trading between Perth and Rotterdam in 1756. [NRS.E504.27.3]

PIETERS, WALSE, master of the Pro Patria van Harlingen trading between Rotterdam and Aberdeen in 1746. [NRS.E504.1.2]

PIETERSDOCHTER, MAERTJE, wife of Matthew Patterson a Scots merchant, testament, 4 February 1643, refers to her brothers Govert Pieterszoon and Willem Pieterszoon. [GAR.ONA.331.62.122]

PIKMAN, ANDREW, a ship's mate, before the Scots Court in Veere, Zealand, in 1728. [NRS.RH11.2.1]

PILBOROUGH, ANDREW, in Edinburgh, son of George Pilborough a merchant in Veere, Zealand, 18 October 1776. [NRS.C22.82/564]

PILLANS, THOMAS, from Edinburgh, was admitted as a citizen of Rotterdam in 1720. [GAR]

PITCAIRN, JOHN, from Scotland, was admitted as a citizen of Rotterdam in 1754. [GAR]

PLENDERLEITH, ALEXANDER, a soldier in Maastricht, Limburg, step-son of Robert Geddes a surgeon apothecary in Edinburgh, a letter, 27 November 1723. [NRS.RH15.70.26]

POIVIR, JOHN, merchant in Middelburg, Zealand, appointed James Oswald a skipper in Kirkcaldy, Fife, as his factor, 27 January 1683. [NRS.B41.7.1/168]

POLLOCK, DAVID, a merchant born in Glasgow, bound for Scotland, testament, 4 April 1630, refers to his wife Annetgen Hendrixdochter. [GAR.ONA.10.183.291]

POLLOCK, JAMES, from Bo'ness. West Lothian, and Catherine Maccallester from Bo'ness, were married in the Scots Kirk in Rotterdam on 25 May 1746. [GAR]

'PONNINCK', JOHN, a Scottish cobbler, and his wife Jannetgen Jacobsdochter, testament, 2 July 1623. [GAR.ONA.104.49.82]

PORTEOUS, ALEXANDER, a Scottish barber in Veere, Zealand, took an Oath of Allegiance to King George II, in Veere, in 1728. [NRS.RH11.2.1]

PORTERFIELD, GEORGE, M.A., an elder of the Scots Church in Rotterdam, 1671-1674. [GAR]

PORTERFIELD, Mrs, in Rotterdam, a letter, 1674. [NRS.RH15.106.171.20]

POTTS, DAVID, from Galloway, was admitted as a citizen of Rotterdam in 1731. [GAR]

PRENTICE, THOMAS, from Edinburgh, was married in Bergen op Zoom, Brabant, on 21 February 1720. [WBA]

PRESCHOUR, MATHEW, a merchant and factor in Brugge, Flanders, 1714. [NRS.RD4.115.945]

PRINGLE, FRANCIS, an MD graduate of the University of Leiden, Holland, applied to become a Fellow of the Royal College of Physicians of Edinburgh in 1704. [NRAS.726.3.12]

PRINGLE, JOHN, an MD graduate of the University of Leiden, Holland, applied to become a Fellow of the Royal College of Physicians of Edinburgh in 1734. [NRAS.726.3.56]; Sir John Pringle, Physician General to HM Forces in Flanders, letters, 1742-1743. [NRS.GD18.5912]

PRINGLE, WILLIAM, a merchant in Surinam, letters, trading with John Drummond of Quarrel, a Scots merchant in Amsterdam, letters, 1725. [NRS.GD24.1.464d]

PRUIST, MATTHIAS, a merchant in Vlissingen, Zealand,1737. [NRS.AC10.263]

PYPER, ALEXANDER, was granted a pass to travel from England to Holland on 4 June 1706. [TNA.SP44.393.2]

PYPER, GEORGE, from Fraserburgh, Aberdeenshire, and Margareta Anderson from Rotterdam, were married in Rotterdam on 12 December 1713. [GAR]; was admitted as a citizen of Rotterdam on 4 October 1715. [GAR]

QUAETT, WILLIAM, burgess of Deventer, Holland, deed, 17 March 1560. [NRS.RDIV.90]

RAE, ALEXANDER, from Haddington, East Lothian, was admitted as a citizen of Rotterdam in 1759. [GAR]

RAE, JAMES, in Major General Stewart's Regiment of Foot in Dutch Service, testament, 13 March1750, Comm. Aberdeen. [NRS]

RAIT, ANDREW, from Aberdeen, and Magdalene Kivit from Dusseldorf, Germany, were married in Rotterdam on 13 March 1695. [GAR]

RAMAGE, ['Rammits'], JOHN, from Culross, Fife, a seaman aboard the New Rotterdam bound for the East Indies, testament, 27 March 1651, refers to his aunt Grietge R

RAMINGS {?}, JOHN, from Dundee, and Elizabeth Watt from Aberdeen, were married in Rotterdam on 3 March 1701. [GAR]

RAMSAY, ALEXANDER, from Edinburgh, married Anna Wark from Edinburgh, in Rotterdam on 1 February 1602. [GAR]

RAMSAY, JAMES, a merchant in Rotterdam, records, 1690s. [NRS.CS228/Misc/29.1]; a ledger 1693. [NRS.CS96.1336]

RAMSAY, ROBERT, fourth son of Robert Ramsay a writer in Dumfries, died in Surinam on 24 April 1818. [BM.3.248]

RAMSAY, WILLIAM, from Newhalls wss admitted as a citizen of Rotterdam on 31 May 1709. [GAR]

RAMSAY, WILLIAM, from the Shetland Islands, and Anna Ramsay from Rotterdam, were married in Rotterdam on 8 January 1710. [GAR]

RAMSAY, WILLIAM, from Edinburgh, was admitted as a citizen of Rotterdam in 1755. [GAR]

RANKIN, GILBERT, from Linlithgow, West Lothian, a seaman under Captain Englebrecht van der See, testament, 27 April 1633, refers to William Boyd living on the Wine Bridge. [GAR.ONA.193.34.48]; testament, 4 December 1634, as above but refers to Scotsman Gilbert Boyd son of William Boyd. [GAR.ONA.195.28.55]

RANKIN, JOHN, and his wife Christina Stirling, from Scotland, a testament, 8 December 1615.

[GAR.ONA.27/185/330]; a 'provoost' or N.C.O. under
Captain Anthony van Sculenburch, a testament, 15 March
1629, refers to his wife Christina Stirling.
[GAR.ONA.128.234.621]

RANNALD, ANDREW, in Cowal ['Cuyl'], a deed, 11 June
1650, refers to his brother John Rannald a seaman under
Admiral de With, to Job Cornelis Rees secretary of the
Admiral, and to his sister Janet Rannald.
[GAR.ONA.211.67.133]

REID, DANIEL, son of John Reid in Cromartie, and Helen
Stuart from Rotterdam, were married in the Scots Kirk in
Rotterdam on 20 January 1723. [GAR] , was admitted as a
citizen of Rotterdam in 1729. [GAR]

REID, WILLIAM, from West Calder, West Lothian, and
Agnes Thomson from Rotterdam, were married in the Scots
Kirk in Rotterdam on 18 February 1705. [GAR]

REIKIE, JOHN, from Edinburgh, and Aaliie Davidson
widow of Alexander Frisingh, were married in Rotterdam on
17 December 1697. [GAR]

RENNALDSON, STEVEN, from Arbroath, Angus, a seaman
under shipmaster Peter Veen of Delfshaven aboard the ship the
St Peter, testament, 25 August 1625, refers to Lyntgen
Stevensdochter van de Gou, also to his own brothers and
sisters in England. [GAR.ONA.187.41.76]; also he as a young
Scot in Naerburg aboard the ship Walcheren, master Jan Mast
of Middelburg, Zealand, bound for the West Indies, testament,
23 December 1628, refers to his landlady Lysbet Jacobsdochter
the widow of Frans Jacobszoon in Mole Lane, Rotterdam.
[GAR.ONA.189/72/108]

RENWICK, JAMES, in Groningen, a letter, 1683.
[NRS.CH3.269.17]

REOCH, GEORGE, a Scotsman, testament, 31 March 1644,
refers to Peter Watson and his wife Catherine Wishart living on
the Schiedam-dyke. [GAR.ONA.205.311.413]

'RHOET, WILLEM', from Edinburgh, a soldier under Captain Nysbee, and Elysbeth Fryer from Edinburgh, widow of Ghysbrecht Michiel, were married in Rotterdam on 23 February 1592. [GAR]

RHYND, ARCHIBALD, from Edinburgh, and Elisabth Zeman from Amsterdam, were married in Rotterdam on 24 July 1718. [GAR]

RHYND, JOHN, an elder of the Scots Church in Rotterdam, 1647-1649. [GAR]

RICKETTS, SAMUEL, a student at Glasgow University in 1816, second son of Samuel Ricketts a merchant in Surinam. [MAGU]

RICKETTS, THOMAS, a student at Glasgow University in 1815, eldest son of Samuel Ricketts a merchant in Surinam. [MAGU]

RIDDELL, JAMES, a merchant in Amsterdam, 23 September 1675. [GAA.NA.3864/46 &228]

RICHARD, ALEXANDER, from Bo'ness, West Lothian, and Jannetje Borrens from Rotterdam, were married in Rotterdam on 13 September 1718. [GAR]

RITCHIE, JOHN, from Bo'ness, West Lothian, was admitted as a citizen of Rotterdam in 1746. [GAR]

ROBERT, ALEXANDER, son of Walter Robert in Carriden, West Lothian, and Jean Corvie, were married in the Scots Kirk in Rotterdam on 26 January 1718. [GAR]

ROBERTSON, or COLLIER, Captain DAVID ALEXANDER, in Bergen-op-Zoom, Brabant, a deed, 1664. [NRS.GD40.1.141]

ROBERTSON, DONALD, son of James Robertson in Perth, and Agnes Coutts from Banff, were married in the Scots Kirk in Rotterdam on 25 December 1754. [GAR]

ROBERTSON, GEORGE, minister in Veere, Zealand, from 1657 to 1660. [SSV.301]

ROBERTSON, JAMES, a seaman from Bo'ness, West Lothian, later in Rotterdam, a letter, 1690. [NRS.CS96/1726/1]

ROBERTSON, JAMES, from the Shetland Islands, and Janet Glent, daughter of James Glent in Rotterdam, were married in Rotterdam on 6 August 1734. [GAR]

ROBERTSON, JOHN, from Edinburgh, and N.Tanneken from Ghent, Flanders, were married in Rotterdam on 10 July 1588. [GAR]

ROBERTSON, ROBERT, from Stirling, widower of Janneken Tourszoon, and Tryntje Jacobs from Rotterdam, were married in Rotterdam on 31 October 1655. [GAR]

ROBERTSON, ROBERT, a young Scotsman, a soldier bound for the East Indies aboard the yacht De Pauw, testament, 15 May 1663, refers to his parents Robert Robertson and Ellen Ramsay. also his brothers and sisters – George, Alexander, John, James, Patrick, Susanna and Helen; also John Forest, a Scotsman and 'provoost' or N.C.O. under Captain Leendart Haecxwant. [GAR.ONA.221.39.145]

ROBERTSON, ROBERT, from Leith, Midlothian, and Gerritge van der Hey from Rotterdam, were married in Rotterdam on 24 March 1704.[GAR]

ROBERTSON, THOMAS, from Falkirk, Stirlingshire, and Marytje de Bruyn, from Vlissingen, Zealand, were married in Rotterdam on 23 April 1754. [GAR]

ROBERTSON, WILLIAM, from Inverness, was admitted as a citizen of Rotterdam in 1729. [GAR]

ROBERTSON, WILLIAM, from Banff, was admitted as a citizen of Rotterdam in 1742. [GAR]

ROBERTSON, WILLIAM, son of Robert Anderson in the Shetland Islands, and Janet, daughter of Alexander Jarvey in Rotterdam, were married in the Scots Kirk in Rotterdam on 6 July 1763. [GAR]

ROBERTSON, WILLIAM, son of John Robertson in Wick, Caithness, and Ann Ridley from Hexham, Northumberland,

England, were married in the Scots Kirk in Rotterdam on 26 July 1769. [GAR]

ROBERTSON, WILLIAM, a merchant in Brussels, bankrupt, papers, 1792-1793. [NRAS.3955.60.3.11]

ROBERTSON, WILLIAM, a planter on Lejuan Island, Essequibo, in 1812. [NRS.RD5.129.194]

ROBINSON, WILLIAM, from Aberdeen, and Johanna Reyniers from Koblenz, Germany, were married in the Scots Kirk in Rotterdam on 31 October 1713. [GAR]

RODGERS, JOHN, son of Richard Rodgers in Bo'ness, West Lothian, and Barbara, daughter of William Keith in Peterhead, Aberdeenshire, were married in the Scots Kirk in Rotterdam on 16 October 1709. [GAR]

RODGER, RALPH, from Glasgow, and Sarah, daughter of Lionel Allan in Rotterdam, were married in the Scots Kirk in Rotterdam on 2 February 1737. [GAR]; was admitted as a citizen of Rotterdam in 1722. [GAR]

ROGER, ROBERT, from Glasgow, and Elisabeth Berrie from Abercorn, West Lothian, were married in Rotterdam on 20 June 1723. [GAR]

ROLLANDS, THOMAS, from Edinburgh, and Tysie Jans, widow of Lauents van Straten, were married in Rotterdam on 28 March 1700. [GAR]

ROLLOK, JAMES, a merchant-burgess of Dundee, 'Portar' or Conservator in Veere, Zealand, 1540s. [OD.78]

ROLLOCK, THOMAS, with wife and children, died in Guadaloupe, French West Indies, before 1656. [GAA.1306.214]

ROSE, ALEXANDER, a surgeon, son of John Rose the Customs Collector of Thurso, Caithness, died in Berbice on 23 August 1802. [EA.4056.02]

ROSS, ANDREW, a skipper from Airth, Stirlingshire, master of the Elphinston, and an assessor at the Scots Court in Veere, Zealand, in 1729, 1731. [NRS.RH11.2.1]

ROSS, ANDREW, fourth son of Hugh Ross of Kerse, died in Berbice on 26 September 1820. [BM.8.482]

ROSS, DAVID, a Scot, was married in Bergen-op-Zoom, Brabant, on 26 October 1698. [WBA]

ROSS, JANE, from Orkney, and George Wood from Belfast, Ireland, were married in Rotterdam on 19 November 1704. [GAR]

ROSS, JOHN, born 1776, died in Nigg, Berbice, on 16 July 1807. [SM.68.958][DPCA.270]

ROUCH, JOHN JAMES, a seaman bound for the East Indies aboard the Honingen Castle, testament, 11 December 1663, refers to his mother Marie Henricx Carif widow of James Rouch living on the Schiedam dyke in the Two Distillerskettle, and to his kin in Aberdour, Fife, also his friend Reynier Heyndricx a seaman. [GAR.ONA.221.90.331]

ROSS, JOHN, born 177, died in Rigg, Berbice on 16 July 1807. [SM.68.958]

ROW, Colonel ARCHIBALD, in Breda, Brabant, a letter, 1702. [NRS.GD124.15.221]

ROWAN, ALEXANDER, son of Alexander Rowan in Dunrossness, in the Shetland Islands, and Mary Body in Rotterdam, were married in the Scots Kirk in Rotterdam on 5 May 1742. [GAR]

RUSSELL, ANDREW, a merchant in Amsterdam, 1675. [GAA.NA.3864/72], an elder of the Scots Church in Rotterdam, 1676-1687; a merchant in Rotterdam, shipped merchandise from Rotterdam aboard the Hannah and Sarah, master John Carter, bound for Boston, New England, 6 September 1686. [NRS.GD1.885.2]

RUSSELL, JAMES, from Scotland, was admitted as a citizen of Rotterdam in 1766. [GAR]

RUSSELL, WILLIAM, from Kirk o' Shotts, Lanarkshire, and Jane Guthrie, widow of Thomas Baylie, were married in the Scors Kirk in Rotterdam on 20 November 1742. [GAR]

RUTHERFORD, DAVID, from Cupar, Fife, an assessor of the Scots Court in Veere, Zealand, in 1731. [NRS.RH11.2.1]

RUTHERFORD, JOHN, son of the laird of Hunthill, at Den Haag, Holland, a bond, 1650. [NRS.GD40.6.10]

RUTHVEN, Captain ALEXANDER, was granted a pass to travel from England to Holland on 18 April 1706. [TNA.SP44.390.433]

'RYPERT, ALEXANDER', from Edinburgh, and Grietgen Pieters, were married in Rotterdam on 25 February 1601. [GAR]

SANDS, JAMES, from "Orthnes" in Scotland, was admitted as a citizen of Rotterdam in 1757. [GAR]

SANDERS, JOHN, from Dundee, a seaman under Captain Jan Jacobszoon van Es, testament, 30 April 1630, refers to Pieter Emmerick's widow Grietge Jans. [GAR.ONA.190.173.263]

SANDERS, WILLIAM, from Dundee, and Gritje Jans from Rotterdam, were married in Rotterdam on 1 September 1630. [GAR]

SANDILANDS, Sir JAMES, from Slamannan, Stirlingshire, a Sergeant Major under Colonel Broggs in the service of the United Provinces, in Amsterdam, a deed, 1629. [NRS.GD84.2.177]

SCHOT, LAURENS JANSZ., and his wife Isabella van Waerdenburch, testament, 11 December 1619. [GAR.ONA.22/64/180]

SCOTT, JAMES, in Haarlem, Holland, son of William Scott in Brazil, 1641. [RGSS.IX.971]

SCOTT, JAMES, in Delft, Holland, 1641. [RGSS.IX.971]

SCOTT, Sir JAMES, born in Rotterdam, was granted denization in England in January 1663. [TNA.Patent Roll, 14 Car ii]

SCOTT, JAMES, in Breda, Brabant, a bill of exchange, 1748. [NRS.GD45.18.949]

SCOTT, JAMES, from Lerwick in the Shetland Islands, and Aaltje van der Wel from Rotterdam, were married in Rotterdam on 7 August 1646. [GAR]

SCOTT, JAMES, from Scotland, was admitted as a citizen of Rotterdam in 1760. [GAR]

SCOTT, JOHN, from St Andrews, Fife, and Elizabeth Andrews from Scotland, were married in Rotterdam on 3 October 1649, [GAR]; a seaman under Captain Jan de Liefde, and his wife Anne Henderson, living in Swan Street, Rotterdam, testament, 6 October 1653. [GAR.ONA.214.107.315]

SCOTT, JOHN, a merchant in Rotterdam, 1714. [NRS.AC9.530]

SCOTT, JOHN, in Brussels, letters, 1722. [NRS.GD158.1968]

SCOTT, JOHN, from Orkney, and Helen Watson, were married in the Scots Kirk in Rotterdam on 5 April 1749. [GAR]

SCOTT, Dr JOHN, late of Batavia, a Crown Charter of the lands of Stewartfield in 1752. [NRS.RGSS.74.101.124]

SCOTT, JOHN, son of John Scott a farmer in Auchinglen, Lanarkshire, died on St Martin's, Dutch West Indies, on 24 March 1807. [SM.69.477]

SCOTT, JOHN, in Demerara, son of John Scott a merchant in Kincardine-on-Forth, Fife, a deed, 20 February 1802. [NRS.RD3.295.657]

SCOTT, LUDOVIC, a Scot, was married in Bergen—op-Zoom, Brabant, on 16 October 1733. [WBA]

SCOTT, THOMAS, from Carriden, West Lothian, and Mary Grindlay from Leith, were married in the Scots Kirk in Rotterdam on 28 May 1749. [GAR]

SCOTT, WILLIAM, a Dutch official in Brazil, a letter, 1641, father of James Scott in Harlem. [RGSS.IX.971]

SCOTT, WILLIAM a Scot, was married in Bergen-op-Zoom, Brabant, on 13 March 1685. [WBA]

SCOTT, WILLIAM, was granted a pass to travel from England to Holland on 29 March 1706. [TNA.SP44.390.410]

SCOULLER, JOHN, son of James Scouller in Bo'ness, West Lothian, and Helen Wright, were married in Rotterdam on 11 February 1705. [GAR]

SCRIMGEOUR, JOHN, was granted a pass to travel from England to Holland on 31 August 1706. [TNA.SP44.393.49]

SEATON, ALEXANDER, graduated from Leiden University, Holland, on 12 November 1597. [UL]

SEGAIT, ALEXANDER, agent for Veere, Zealand, in 1577. [SSN.89/93]

SELLER, ALEXANDER, from Aberdeen, was admitted as a citizen of Rotterdam on 15 December 1718. [GAR]

SENSERFE, WALTER, born in Rotterdam of Scottish parents, a grant of denization in England on 26 September 1662. [TNA.Patent Roll, 14 Car ii]

SETON, GEORGE, Earl of Winton, in Rotterdam, a letter, 1669. [NRS.GD1.1192.10]

SETON, Sir HENRY, Captain on military service in Holland, was granted the lands of Colbegg on 23 February 1753. [NRS.RGSS.101/159]

SETON, JAMES, from Buckhaven, Fife, and Grisel Pottinger from Bressay in the Shetland Islands, were married in the Scots Kirk in Rotterdam on 22 May 1756. [GAR]

SHAIRP, THOMAS, nephew of Thomas Shairp of Houston, Renfrewshire, bound for Leiden, a letter from Rotterdam dated 21 September 1717. [NRS.GD30.2278]

SHAIRP, WALTER, a Captain of the Scots Fusiliers Regiment in Flanders, a deed of factory, 1697. [NRS.GD30.461]

SHAND, GEORGE, a merchant from Aberdeen, before the Scots Court in Veere, Zealand, in 1738, accused of selling stockings in Middelburg, Zealand, instead of in the Staple Port of Veere, [NRS.RH11.2.1]

SHANTON, ALEXANDER, from Kintyre, Argyll, and Margaret Wart widow of James Gordon, were married in the Scots Kirk in Rotterdam on 12 February 1746. [GAR]

SHARP, DUNCAN, from Campbeltown, Argyll, and Janet Ferguson from Ieperen, Flanders, were married in the Scots Kirk in Rotterdam on 12 February 1774. [GAR]

SHARP, JOHN, from Alloa, Clackmannan, and Esther Harwar [?] from Tulliallan, Stirlingshire, were married in the Scots Kirk in Rotterdam on 16 February 1702. [GAR]

SHEARER, CHARLES, from Stirling, a burgess of Edinburgh, residing in Dort, Holland, a bond, 1627; documents, 1631-1649. [NRS.GD30.1214, 1225; NRS.B66.25.506.1-11]

SHEARER, JAMES, son of Robert Shearer, a poultryman in Stirling, sometime in Holland, 1640. [NRS.B66.25.506.1-11]

SHEARER, JOHN, a Scot from Dort, Holland, living by 't Grote Hooft, bound for Scotland, a testament, 13 January 1635, refers to Christine Jardine, widow of Andrew Hay from Dort, living on the Rietdike in Tiel, Gelderland, Adam

Leendertszoon on Lindesgraft, Isaac Conijn, Jan Blom, Coenraet Dammisz, and Staes Reynierszoon. [GAR.ONA.195.47.86]

SHEARER, WILLIAM, from Bo'ness, West Lothian, was admitted as a citizen of Rotterdam on 7 November 1719. [GAR]

SHEBBERY, SANDER, from Aberdeen, and Maritje Jans widow of Dirk van Gelder from Rotterdam, were married in Rotterdam on 25 July 1700. [GAR]

SHEPHERD, MAGNUS, son of William Shepherd in Bo'ness, West Lothian, and Margaret Thomson widow of Alexander Dunsager, were married in the Scots Kirk in Rotterdam on 11 May 1748. [GAR]

SHIELDS, JOHN, son of Andrew Shields, an apprentice to John Gilmour a weaver in Paisley, Renfrewshire, absconded and joined General Colyer's Regiment bound for Holland in 1747. [NRS.AC10.325]

SIBBALD, or WILLIAMSON, ARCHIBALD, a Scottish gunner under Captain Teunis Condee, testament, 3 September 1636, refers to Andrew Sanderson and his wife Lijsbet Gijsbertsdochter. [GAR.ONA.196.175.317]

SIBBALD, JOHN, a Scot, was married in Bergen-op-Zoom, Brabant, on 25 September 1733. [WBA]

SIBBETT, PETER, a Scot, was married in Bergen-op- Zoom, Brabant, on 12 January 1702. [WBA]

SIMPSON, JOHN, a merchant in Amsterdam, 1714; 1720; 1723. [GAA.NA.8571/579; 8599.818] [NRS.AC9.530]

SIMS, GEORGE, a Scots sailor in the service of the Dutch East India Company, bound aboard Den Duyvel van Delff for the East Indies, a promissory note dated 18 December 1619 refers to his sisters Margaret Sims and Catherine Jansdochter, also his landlady Maetgen Gerrits and her daughter Anna Jansdochter. [GAR.ONA.37/146/317]

SIMSON, ALEXANDER, from Aberdeen, was admitted as a citizen of Rotterdam in 1748. [GAR]

SIMSON, DAVID, from Bo'ness, West Lothian, and Willemi Christiaens widow of Jan Jacobs van Agten, were married in Rotterdam on 4 June 1712 in Rotterdam. [GAR]

SIMPSON, GEORGE, from Scotland, was admitted as a citizen of Rotterdam in 1769. [GAR]

SIMSON, ROBERT, a resident of Brugge, Flanders, a charter, 1576. [NRS.GD1.1088.31]

SINCLAIR, EDWARD, in Kersewood, and Janet McGillvary in Rotterdam, were married in the Scots Kirk in Rotterdam on 5 June 1776. [GAR]

SINCLAIR, GEORGE, from Elgin, Morayshire, and Maria Thomson from Viljmen, were married in Rotterdam on 14 August 1712. [GAR]

SINCLAIR, JAMES, son of Alexander Sinclair in Kersewood, and Agnes Berrie, daughter of Andrew Berrie in Rotterdam, were married in the Scots Kirk in Rotterdam on 15 June 1743. [GAR]; was admitted as a citizen of Rotterdam in 1754. [GAR]

SINCLAIR, JOHN, from Edinburgh, and Margarieta Ros from Rotterdam, were married in Rotterdam on 13 September 1705. [GAR]

SINCLAIR, JOHN, in Ghent, Flanders, a letter, 1712. [NRS.GD406.1.5814]

SINCLAIR, WILLIAM, from 'Brag', was admitted as a citizen of Rotterdam on 8 November 1717. [GAR]

SINCLAIR, WILLIAM, a medical student in Leiden, Holland, letters, 1737-1738. [NRS.GD136.376]

SKENE, ANDREW, a merchant burgess of Aberdeen and factor in Veere, Zealand, husband of Christine Skene, and father of Robert Skene, a land grant in Aberdeenshire, 5 May 1665. [NRS.RGSS.XI.751]

SKENE, ANDREW, of Pitmuckstone, factor at Veere, Zealand, husband of Isobel Donaldson, dead by 1702. [NRS.RD2.86.2.35]

SKEEN, FRANCIS, in Ghent, Flanders, a letter, 1712. [NRAS.3955.897.118]

SKENE, ROBERT, in Amsterdam, a letter, 1669. [NRAS.897.99]

SKINNER, JAMES, from Montrose, Angus, was admitted as a citizen of Rotterdam in 1735. [GAR]

SMALL, DAVID, from Anstruther, Fife, a seaman aboard the Zeelandia commander Jan van Nes, testament, 3 November 1672, refers to his nephew William Small and his wife Catherine Johnson, another David Small and Greta Andrews living in Anstruther. [GAR.ONA.921.270.845]

SMEER, FRANCIS, master of the Maria van Amsterdam trading between Perth and Bilbao in 1760. [NRS.E504.27.3]

SMITH, CHARLES, from Scotland, was admitted as a citizen of Rotterdam in 1770. [GAR]

SMITH, DANIEL, from Aberdeen, was admitted as a citizen of Rotterdam in 1750. [GAR]

SMITH, DANIEL, from Scotland, was admitted as a citizen of Rotterdam in 1771. [GAR]

SMITH, HENRY, a Scot, was married in Bergen op Zoom, Brabant, on 17 November 1633. [WBA]

SMITH, HENRY, from Bo'ness, West Lothian, and Elizabeth de Bruyn from Rotterdam, were married in Rotterdam on 25 June 1715. [GAR]

SMITH, JAMES, from Leith, Midlothian, and Grietgen Thomas from Rotterdam, were married in Rotterdam on 8 June 1664. [GAR]

SMITH, JOHN, a young Scotsman, a seaman under Captain Jan van Nes, testament, 26 August 1641, refers to Elisabeth Duncan widow of John Smith, mother of John Smith the young Scots seaman, living on the Schiedam dyke in Rotterdam. [GAR.ONA.202.224.285]

SMITH, JOHN, a drummer of Colonel Bridges' Regiment of Foot in Flanders, married Esther, daughter of James Crawford a merchant in Lanark, in December 1692. A process of adherence, 1706. [NRS.CC8.6.138]

SMITH, JOHN, a surgeon, died in Berbice on 14 December 1822. [SM.91.519]

SMITH, THOMAS, a Scot, was married in Bergen op Zoom, Brabant, on 24 April 1630. [WBA]

SMITH, THOMAS, from Dundee, and Mary Grant from Aberdeen, were married in Rotterdam on 16 September 1708. [GAR]

SMITH, THOMAS, from Scotland, was admitted as a citizen of Rotterdam in 1763. [GAR]

SMITH, WILLIAM, from the Shetland Islands, and Mary Mitchell widow of Peter Higgins, were married in the Scots Kirk in Rotterdam on 8 August 1733. [GAR]

SMITH, WILLIAM, a merchant in Amsterdam, father of Helen Smith, born in Amsterdam in 1838, buried in Dundee on 17 May 1840. [Dundee, Howff MI]

SMOLLETT, JAMES, a student in Leiden, Holland, a letter, 1704. [NRS.RH15.31.11]

SMYTH, THOMAS, a burgess of Peebles, a bond with Adriaan and Cornelius Lampsins of Middelburg, Zealand, and Vlissingen, Zealand, 1649. [NRS.PA7.6]

SNYPE, ANDREW, minister of the Scots Kirk in Veere, Zealand, from 1660 until his death in 1686. [SSV.303]

SOMERVILLE, WILLIAM, born 1611, from Renfrew, shipmaster of the Paul of Rotterdam, a witness, April 1644. [TNA.HCA.59.117]

SOMMERS, JOHN, from Aberdeen, and Amelia Thomson from Leith, Midlothian, were married in Rotterdam on 16 January 1707. [GAR]

SONMANS, JOHANNA, eldest daughter of Stron Sonmans in Rotterdam, title to lands in East New Jersey, 1683-1685. [NRS.RH15.131]

SPANG, WILLIAM, minister at Veere, Zealand, 1634. [SHS.6/3]; a letter, 1652. [NRS.GD40.2.5.43]

SPEIR, ALEXANDER, the younger, factor and merchant at Veere, Zealand, 1634, son of Alexander Speir a merchant burgess of Edinburgh. [SHS.6/3]

SPENCER, JOHN, a Scot, was married in Halsteren, Brabant, on 4 May 1676. [WBA]

STAVINES, CORNELIUS, of Zealand, was admitted as a burgess and guilds-brother of Aberdeen on 13 March 1639. [ABR]

STAY, ALEXANDER, from Edinburgh, was admitted as a citizen of Rotterdam in 1764. [GAR]

STEDMAN, CHARLES, from Bo'ness, West Lothian, was admitted as a citizen of Rotterdam in 1744. [GAR]

STEEL, JAMES, from Irvine, Ayrshire, and Ann Taylor daughter of Robert Taylor in Rotterdam, were married in the Scots Kirk in Rotterdam on 2 October 1755. [GAR]; was admitted as a citizen of Rotterdam in 1759. [GAR]

STEEN, DAVID, from Stirling, and Helena Brocks from Edinburgh, were married in Rotterdam on 21 June 1620. [GAR]

STEEN, JOHN, a Scot, was married in Bergen op Zoom, Brabant, on 31 March 1637. [WBA]

STENHOUSE, ["STENNIS"], ROBERT, from Dumfries, was admitted as a citizen of Rotterdam in 1739. [GAR]

STEPHENSON, JAMES, from Aberdeen, was admitted as a citizen of Rotterdam in 1773. [GAR]

STEVENS, DAVID, from Aberdeen, and Aefge Jans from Bergen, were married in Rotterdam on 21 February 1621. [GAR]

STEVENSON, MARTIN, merchant burgess of Edinburgh, debtor to Henry Vrymoet, merchant in Dordrecht, Holland, 1665. [ECA.MBIII.50/2207]

STEVENSON, PATRICK, son of William Stevenson in Glasgow, and Margaret Wallace in Rotterdam, were married in the Scots Kirk in Rotterdam on 18 June 1735. [GAR]

STEWART, ALEXANDER, in Ostend, Flanders, a letter,1794. [NRAS.3955.60.1.409]

STEWART, C. W., in Bergen op Zoom, Brabant, a letter, 1732. [NRS.GD1.407.24]

STEWART, DUNCAN, from Scotland, was admitted as a citizen of Rotterdam in 1763. [GAR]

STEWART, GILBERT, in Scotland, formerly a merchant in Rotterdam, a deed, 1702. [NRS.RD4.90.234]

STEWART, JAMES, from Grenada, died in Demerara on 1 February 1791. [SM.53.203]

STEWART, JOHN, a merchant in Veere, Zealand, 1754. [NRAS.2236.14]

STEWART, JOHN, from Glasgow, was admitted as a citizen of Rotterdam in 1790. [GAR]

STEWART, ROBERT, a merchant in Veere, Zealand, a deed, 1702. [NRS.RD4.90.394]

STEWART, ROBERT, a merchant in Rotterdam, was granted the lands of Muriehall on 14 September 1703. [NRS.RGSS.79.257]

STEWART, Sir WILLIAM, of Houstoun, the Scottish Ambassador to Flanders in 1594. [NRS.GD30.117]

STEWART, WILLIAM, from Bo'ness, West Lothian, and Janet Ogilvy from Rotterdam, were married in the Scots Kirk in Rotterdam on 5 February 1708. [GAR]

STEWART, WILLIAM, from Jamaica, married Maria Odelia van Hoogement, daughter of Gerevid van Hoogement a merchant in La Rochelle, France, in Edinburgh on 3 January 1780. [Edinburgh Marriage Register]

STEWART, ..., a Scot, was married in Bergen op Zoom, Brabant, on 18 May 1597. [WBA]

STIRLING, JAMES, a merchant in Edinburgh, was granted a pass to travel from England to Holland on 18 June 1706. [TNA.SP44.393.9]

STIRLING, ROBERT, from Edinburgh, and Adriana van der Velde widow of Bernard Vishoueck in Schiedam, Holland, were married in Rotterdam on 14 January 1601. [GAR]

STOUT, HENRY, from Inverness, and Elizabeth Boulton from Sunderland in England, were married in Rotterdam on 16 December 1753. [GAR]

STOUT, THOMAS, from Dunrossness in the Shetland Islands, and Anna van der Bouw, from Rotterdam, were married in the Scots Kirk in Rotterdam on 23 April 1768; later he, now a widower, married Catherine Watson from Rotterdam, in the Scots Kirk in Rotterdam on 10 December 1768. [GAR]

STRACHAN, DAVID, a student in Leiden, Holland, a letter, 1719. [NRS.GD45.14.838]

STRACHAN, JAMES, a merchant in Veere, Zealand, 1754. [NRAS.2236.14]

STRACHAN, Captain JOHN, son of Thomas Strachan and his wife Helen Scott in Forgan, Fife, died in Flanders before September 1600. [MSC.II.54]

STRACHAN, JOHN, Scotsman, a 'provoost' or an N.C.O. under Captain Pieter van Allevrunden, testament, 11 June 1637, refers to William Roberts, a Scotsman, and his wife Janet Robertsdochter living in High Street, Rotterdam. [GAR.ONA.197.181.185]

STRACHAN, WILLIAM, from Banff, was admitted as a citizen of Rotterdam in 1754. [GAR]; formerly a merchant in Rotterdam, later residing in Banff, Scotland, a testament, 22 July 1777, Comm. Aberdeen. [NRS]

STRANG, LAURENCE, son of George Strang in the Shetland Islands, and Elizabeth Gillon from Bo'ness, West Lothian, were married in the Scots Kirk in Rotterdam on 20 May 1716. [GAR]

STRATH, THOMAS, a Scot, was married in Bergen op Zoom, Brabant, on 18 July 1736. [WBA]

STREETMAN, JOHN, from Bo'ness, West Lothian, was admitted as a citizen of Rotterdam in 1727. [GAR]

STRONG, CORNELIUS, from Dunrossness in the Shetland Islands, and Catherine Nielson from Lerwick also in the Shetland Islands, were married in the Scots Kirk in Rotterdam on 20 April 1771. [GAR]

STRONG, JOHN, from Fair Isle, Shetland Islands, was admitted as a citizen of Rotterdam in 1745. [GAR]

STROOBAND, ABRAM, factor for William and John Davidson merchants in Rotterdam, before the Scots Court in Veere, Zealand, in 1736. [NRS.RH11.2.1]

STUART, ALEXANDER, from Banff, was admitted as a citizen of Rotterdam in 1733. [GAR]

STUART, CHARLES, Depute Lord Conservator of the Privileges of the Scots Nation in the Netherlands, In 1738 he was appointed as an executor of the will of Reverend Charles Jervay minister of the Scots Kirk in Rotterdam. [NRS.RH11.2.1]; He was appointed as Conservator in 1760, and died in 1761 [GAR].

STUART, JAMES, and Elizabeth Murdoch, were married in the Scots Reformed Church in Rotterdam on 14 July 1793. [NRAS.1141.8.250]

STUART, JOHN, from Perth, and Lena Hannah from Wigtown, were married in Rotterdam on 16 December 1712. [GAR]

STUART, JOHN, clerk of the Scots Court in Veere, Zealand, in 1735. [NRS.RH11.2.1]

STUART, JOHN, born 1767 in Forgue, Aberdeenshire, a planter in the Dutch colonies of Surinam and Essequibo by 1799, died in Trinidad in 1808.

STUPART, JAMES, from Alloa, Clackmannanshire, and Jannetje Wilson from Rotterdam, were married in Rotterdam on 25 June 1724. [GAR]; was admitted as a citizen of Rotterdam in 1730 [GAR]

SUERD, SAARNES, a Dutchman, shipmaster burgess of 'Bolliswart', a deed, 1558. [NRS.RD1.113]

SUTHERLAND, JAMES, a Scot, was married in Bergen op Zoom, Brabant, on 20 June 1778. [WBA]

SUTHERLAND, JOHN, a servant, was granted a pass to travel from England to Holland on 18 April 1706. [TNA.SP44.390.433]

SUTHERLAND, JOHN, from Caithness, and Mary Sutherland from Tiel, Gelderland, were married in the Scots Kirk in Rotterdam on 27 October 1742. [GAR]

SUTTIE, PATRICK, factor in Veere, Zealand, 1633. [SHS.6/3]

SWINTON, GILBERT, a Scot, was married in Bergen op Zoom, Brabant, on 27 December 1634. [WBA]

SYDSERFE, GEORGE, of Rouchlay, was appointed minister at Veere, Zealand, in 1625. [SSN.166]

SYMMER, ..., in Ghent, Flanders, a letter, 1712. [NRS.GD406.71.5856]

TAYLOR, ALEXANDER, son of Alexander Taylor in Newhills, Aberdeenshire, and Agnes Dines from Tranent, East Lothian, were married in the Scots Kirk in Rotterdam on 14 July 1711. [GAR]

TAYLOR, ANDREW, from Edinburgh, and Naomi Christins from Yarmouth, England, were married in Rotterdam on the 9 May 1753. [GAR]

TAYLOR, DAVID, a merchant in Middelburg, Zealand, 1763. [NRS.SC20.36.11]

TAYLOR, GEORGE, a merchant in Amsterdam, 1720; 2 December 1721. [GAA.NA.8571/1189 &1455; NA.8589/1207]; letter, 1721. [NRS.GD164.1650]

TAYLOR, JOHN, a seaman under Lieutenant Admiral Maerten Harperszoon Tromp, testament, 5 April 1641, refers to Gilbert Grant, his brother–in-law, living in Paeuwes Street, Rotterdam. [GAR.ONA.385.1110.24]

TAYLOR, JOHN, from Bo'ness, West Lothian, was admitted as a citizen of Rotterdam in 1745. [GAR]

TAYLOR, ROBERT, from Queensferry, West Lothian, and Isabel Keill, were married in the Scots Kirk in Rotterdam on 23 September 1725. [GAR]

TAYLOR, WILLIAM, from Daviot, Inverness-shire, was admitted as a citizen of Rotterdam in 1777. [GAR]

TENNANT, SMART, an Official Factor of the Scots Staple at Veere, Zealand, in 1740; a merchant in Veere and owner of a tenement of Parliament Square, Edinburgh. [NRS.RH11.2.1; E109.8][SSV.261]

TENYSON, JACOB, master of the Crab of Hoorn, Holland, which arrived in the Clyde in May 1627. [GBR]

TERRER, THOMAS, a Scotsman, a seaman aboard the Mastricht bound for the East Indies, testament, 6 January 1642, refers to Jan Janszoon and his wife Francijntge Maertens. [GAR.ONA.130.2.5]

THOMAS, WILLIAM, a widower from Bo'ness, West Lothian, and Lena Jacobs Lighart, were married in Rotterdam on 16 June 1711. [GAR]

THOMSON, ALEXANDER, from Culross, Fife, and Ann Dod from Sunderland, England, were married in the Scots Kirk in Rotterdam on 15 September 1759. [GAR]

THOMSON, CORNELIUS, a factor in Holland, 1686; a merchant in Rotterdam, 1687. [NRS.AC7.7/8]

THOMSON, DAVID, a Scot, was married in Bergen-op-Zoom, Brabant, on 16 March 1655. [WBA]

THOMSON, GEORGE, a Scotsman, aged 45, a seaman under Vice Admiral Witte Corneliszoon de With, testament, 26 July 1640, refers to a Scottish sweetheart Lijsbet Jansdochter, and James Robertson a Scot. [GAR.ONA.200.248.362]

THOMSON, GEORGE, from Leith, Midlothian, was admitted as a citizen of Rotterdam on 24 April 1709. [GAR]

THOMSON, GEORGE, from Scotland, was admitted as a citizen of Rotterdam in 1757. [GAR]

THOMSON, JAMES, from Edinburgh, and Josyntje Cok from Klasswael, were married in Rotterdam on 2 May 1653. [GAR]

THOMSON, JAMES, a merchant in Rotterdam, son of Thomas Thomson a merchant burgess of Linlithgow, West Lothian, a deed, 1692. [NRAS.4092.17]

THOMSON, JAMES, from Stirlingshire, and Mary Wright, were married in the Scots Kirk in Rotterdam on 9 October 1715. [GAR]

THOMPSON, JOHN, a Scot, was married in Bergen op Zoom, Brabant, on 3 November 1621 [WBA]

THOMSON, JOHN, a Scotsman, a seaman under Admiral Tromp, a deed, 24 February 1641, refers to John Robertson, a tailor living on the Schiedam dyke, and his sisters Janet and Helen Thomson in Musselburgh, Midlothian. [GAR.ONA.201.204.269]

THOMSON, JOHN, an elder of the Scots Church in Rotterdam, 1671-1674. [GAR]

THOMPSON, JOHN, a servant, was granted a pass to travel from England to Holland on 5 April 1706. [TNA.SP44.390.415a]

THOMSON, RICHARD, from Denny, Stirlingshire, and Agnes Walker widow of John Shaw, were married in the Scots Kirk in Rotterdam on 16 January 1709. [GAR]

THOMPSON, ROBERT, a Scot, was married in Bergen op Zoom, Brabant, on 3 November 1621. [WBA]

THOMSON, THOMAS, from the Shetland Islands, and Elizabeth Geln from Rotterdam, were married in the Scots Kirk in Rotterdam on 19 December 1733. [GAR]

THOMSON, THOMAS, from Scotland, was admitted as a citizen of Rotterdam in 1775. [GAR]

THOMSON, WILLIAM, from Perth, a tailor in Veere, Zealand, inventory, 18 June 1546. [GAV.Inv.920]

THOMSON, WILLIAM, Canon of the Church of our Lady at Antwerpen, Flanders, was sent to Edinburgh to persuade the Scots to establish Antwerpen as their Staple Port in the Low Countries in 1539. [SSN.54]

THOMSON, WILLIAM, from Bo'ness, West Lothian, and Maertje Jans from Schiedam, were married in Rotterdam on 28 December 1653. [GAR]

THOMSON, WILLIAM, a Scot, was married in Bergen op Zoom, Brabant, on 23 March 1707. [WBA]

THOMSON, WILLIAM, from Edinburgh, was admitted as a citizen of Rotterdam in 1721. [GAR]

TODD, GEORGE, a merchant from Edinburgh, was admitted as a burger of Antwerpen, Flanders, in 1545 [SAA]

TORRY, ROBERT, from Leith, Midlothian, and Anneken Luynzeel, were married in Rotterdam on 26 January 1620. [GAR]

TULISON, MARTIN, an innkeeper in Rotterdam, an account book, 1708-1712. [NRS.CS96.1945]

TULLOCH, HUBERT, a Scot, was married in Bergen-op-Zoom, Brabant, on 19 October 1768. [WBA]

TULLOCH, WILLIAM, from Scotland, was admitted as a citizen of Rotterdam in 1747. [GAR]

TURING, JAMES, a factor at the Scottish Staple of Veere , Zealand, in 1736. In 1738 he was appointed as an executor of the will of Reverend Charles Jervay minister of the Scots Kirk in Rotterdam. [NRS.RH11.2.1]

TURING, ..., daughter of James Henry Turing, was born in Rotterdam on 25 June 1822. [SM.90.267]

TURNBULL, JOHN, a merchant in Edinburgh, was granted a pass to travel from England to Holland on 18 June 1706. [TNA.SP44.393.9]

TURNBULL, PETER, a merchant from Aberdeen, an assessor of the Scots Court in Veere, Zealand, 1728, 1738. [NRS.RH1.2.1]

TURNER, ANDREW, a merchant in Holland, and William Turner, were heirs to John Turner, a merchant in Danzig, 1690. [NRS.GD244.1.235]

TWITZES, HENDRICK, master of the Young Yeates of Fricsland trading between Aberdeen and Rotterdam in 1749. [NRS.E504.1.3]

TYTLER, CHARLES, from Midmar, and Elizabeth Miller from Hertenbosch, Brabant, were married in the Scots Church in Rotterdam on 30 January 1740. [GAR]

URE, JAMES, an elder of the Scots Church in Rotterdam, 1663-1663. [GAR]

URQUHART, JAMES, in Arnhem, Gelderland, a letter, 1702. [NRS.GD220.5.29]

URQUHART, Sir THOMAS, in Middelburg, Zealand, a letter, 1655. [NRS.GD26.13.267]

VALENTINE, JOHN, emigrated via Amsterdam aboard the Philadelphia Packet, master Edward Rice, bound for Philadelphia, Pennsylvania, in 1791, [Penn.Archives.2nd.series, vol.xvii]

VAN BARTHINE, VENDILENA, spouse of Sir Walter Riddell of that Ilk, Captain in the service of the United Provinces, parents of Jonathan Frederick Riddell and Margaret Riddell, testament of Sir W. Riddell, 1676, Comm. Edinburgh. [NRS]

VAN CHARANT, GABRIEL, a factor, 1741. [NRS.AC9.1519]

VAN DER BURG, FRANCIS, a councillor and recorder in Dordrecht, Holland, relict of Anna Davidson, a deed, 1705. [NRS.RD2.90.363]

VAN DER BURG, JOHN, an advocate in Holland, a deed, 1705. [NRS.RD2.90.363]

VAN DER HAYDEN, JEAN, wife of James Coutts in Montrose, Angus, and mother of Hercules Coutts, born 1714, a merchant in Maryland before 1751. [NRS.RD4.177.298]

VAN DER HEIDEN and DRUMMOND, merchants in Amsterdam, deeds, 1705. [NRS.RD2.90.83/809; RD2.90.198/660; RD3.105.134]

VAN DER MULES, JOHN, a merchant in Leiden, Holland, 1677. [NRS.AC7.4]

VAN DER SYPE, Mr, a deed, 1715. [NRS.RD4.116.700]

VAN DER VATER, JOHN, a bookseller in Utrecht, deeds, 1705, 1715. [NRS.RD4.97.822; RD3.145.195]

VAN DOENGHEN, GERTRUDE, relict of George Douglas a routmaster, a bond, 26 August 1661. [NRS.RD4.3.154]

VAN DOORN, ROMBOUT, a merchant in Vlissingen, Zealand, 1742. [NRS.AC9.1522]

VAN EER, GILBERT JANSZOON, [Gilbert Johnson from Ayr?], in Scotland, a seaman under Captain Joris Janszoon Munnick, testament, 7 October 1630, refers to Robbrecht Joriszoon and his wife Maria Willemsdochter. [GAR.ONA.190.295.459]

VAN EGMONT, JEUNIS, a merchant in Rotterdam, 1778. [NRS.CS16.1.173/448]

VAN GHENT, ELISABETH WILHELMINA, wife of Colonel George Lawder of Restalrig, accused of adultery in 1692. [NRS.CC8.5.1]

VAN HUISEN, JAN SIMON, master of the Green Dragon of Amsterdam, was admitted as a burgess of Aberdeen on 15 July 1623. [ABR]

VAN HOOGEMENT, MARIA ODELIA, daughter of Gerevid van Hoogement a merchant in La Rochelle, France, married William Stewart from Jamaica in Edinburgh on 3 January 1780. [Edinburgh Marriage Register]

VAN MANES, A., in Rotterdam, a deed, 1715. [NRS.RD2.104.673]

VAN MEIN, HALLERT, a merchant in Rotterdam, 1714. [NRS.AC9.530]

VAN RAXTELL, Mr in Rotterdam, a deed, 1715. [NRS.RD3.144.7]

VAN RIXTER, JAN, in Haarlem, Holland, trading with Andrew Russell a merchant in Rotterdam, papers, 1683-1685. [NRS.RH15.471.550]

VAN SCOONENBERG, JAN, master of the Jonge Nelleta, trading between Rotterdam and Perth in 1747. [NRS.E504.27.1]

VAN WYNGAARDEN, SOPHIA, widow of George Gregorie a Scottish factor in Veere, Zealand, petitioned the Scots Court of Veere in 1731; also in 1739 regarding their mutual will subscribed to in Middelburg, Zealand, on 18 October 1736 by Daniel Zutterman a notary public. [NRS.RH11.2.1]

VASS, JOHN, a Scot, was married in Bergen op Zoom, Brabant, on 28 September1714. [WBA]

VASS, JOHN, a Scot, was married in Bergen op Zoom, Brabant, on 21 August 1720. [WBA]

VEDER, ROBERT, from Lerwick in the Shetland Islands, and Helen Young, from Dunrossness in the Shetland Islands, were married in the Scots Kirk in Rotterdam on 30 December 1752. [GAR]

VER BRUGH, DIONNIS JANESSEN, a flax merchant in Rotterdam, testament, 29 February 1676, Comm. Edinburgh. [NRS]

VERTUE, WILLIAM, a skipper from Alloa, Stirlingshire, and an assessor of the Scots Court in Veere, Zealand, in 1736. [NRS.RH11.2.1]

VETCH, SAMUEL, born 9 December 1668 in Edinburgh, son of William Vetch a Presbyterian minister and a Covenanter who fled to the Netherlands in 1683. Samuel, and his brother William, were educated at the University of Utrecht. Samuel accompanied William of Orange to England in 1688, later was appointed an officer of the Royal Scots Dragoons and fought in Flanders. In 1698 he joined the Darien Expedition, but on its failure settled in New York. Samuel married Margaret, daughter of Robert Livingston, and became a merchant in Albany and in Boston. He participated in military expedition which captured Port Royal, Acadia, [later Annapolis, Nova Scotia], and served as Governor of Nova Scotia from 1710 to 1717. Samuel Vetch died in London in 1732. [SCS][NEHGS]

VINCENT, WILLIAM, a Scot, his testament dated 12 October 1620 refers to his wife Janet Patrick, his son George Williamson and daughter Mary Williamson. [GAR.ONA.102.71.100]

VLIELAND, ENGEL ARENDS, master of the Frow Anna van Amsterdam trading between Amsterdam and Perth in 1764. [NRS.E504.27.5]

VYSER, THOMAS CLAASE, a Dutch harpooner aboard the Peggy of Glasgow, whaling off Greenland in 1751. [NRS.E508.48.8]

WADDELL, JAMES, from Bo'ness, West Lothian, was admitted as a citizen of Rotterdam in 1740. [GAR]

WALKER, JOHN, from Aberdeen, was admitted as a citizen of Rotterdam in 1753. [GAR]

WALKER, MATTHEW, from Edinburgh, and Lysbeth Tote from Rotterdam, were married in Rotterdam on 17 August 1723. [GAR]

WALKER, WILLIAM, from Edinburgh, was admitted as a citizen of Rotterdam in 1751. [GAR]

WALKER, Reverend WILLIAM, from Edinburgh, and Elizabeth Lawson from Banff, were married in the Scots Kirk in Rotterdam on 21 November 1767. [GAR]

WALKER, ..., a young girl from Scotland living in Schilderstraet, Rotterdam, testament, 12 June 1639, refers to John Dingwall and Janneken Craviet. [GAR.ONA.302.319.639]

WALLACE, Colonel JAMES, an elder of the Scots Church in Rotterdam, 1676-1678. [GAR]

WALLACE, JOHN, Deputy Conservator at Veere, Zealand, in 1613. [SSN.154/158/159]

WALLACE, SAMUEL, a merchant in Veere, Zealand, 1641. [SHS.6/3]; a merchant in Veere, son of John Wallace the deputy Conservator of the Scots Privileges in the Low Countries, 1 July 1646. [RGSS.IX,1676]

WALLACE, WILLIAM, an elder of the Scots Church in Rotterdam, 1660-1666. [GAR]

WALLIS, ALEXANDER, was granted a pass to travel from England to Holland on 14 December 1705. [TNA.SP44.394.1]

'WALRACKT', ROBERT, a Scots mariner, living on the Schiedam dyke, testament, 9 February 1651, refers to his wife Grietgen Jaersdochter and her child John Robertson. [GAR.ONA.116.89.148]

WALTERSON, JOHN, from Edinburgh, a soldier bound for the East Indies under shipmaster Pieter Corneliszoon, testament, 14 February 1631. [GAR.ONA.191/117/146]

WANT, WILLIAM, a young man from Linlithgow, West Lothian, a seaman under Vice Admiral de With, testament, 15 April 1653, refers to his brother John Want and his mother Janet Thomson in Linlithgow. [GAR.ONA.214.50.156]

WARDLAW, JAMES, an elder of the Scots Church in Rotterdam, 1661-1664. [GAR]

WARTLAW, ["WARTHALL"], MARY, from Scotland, was admitted as a citizen of Rotterdam in 1768. [GAR]

WAT, ANDREW, a shipmaster from Aberdeen, was appointed as an assessor of the Scots Court in Veere, Zealand, in 1738. [NRS.RH11.2.1]

WATT, JOHN, from Cupar in Fife, and Lilian Thomson, were married in the Scots Kirk in Rotterdam on 9 February 1716. [GAR]

WATER, JOHN, from Tweedmouth, Berwickshire, and Lydia Baker from Bristol, England, were married in Rotterdam on 7 July 1682. [GAR]

WATSON, GEORGE, from Edinburgh, was admitted as a citizen of Rotterdam in 1746. [GAR]

WATSON, GEORGE, from Aberdeen, was admitted as a citizen of Rotterdam in 1769. [GAR]

WATSON, JACK, aboard the Black Knight under master Claes Corneliszoon 't Meickmeisje bound for the West Indies, a testament, 24 January 1628, refers to William Johnston a Scotsman. [GAR.ONA.128.183.496]

WATSON, JAMES, a Scots burgess of Brugge, Flanders, 1540. [SSN.56]

WATSON, JAMES, died on St Martins, Dutch West Indies, on 14 June 1804. [SM.65.644]

WATSON, JANET, from Edinburgh, was admitted as a citizen of Rotterdam on 19 February 1711. [GAR]

WATSON, JOHN, from Edinburgh, and Janet Giles from Rotterdam, were married in the Scots Kirk in Rotterdam on 15 June 1743. [GAR]

WATSON, ROBERT, from Scotland, was admitted as a citizen of Rotterdam in 1747. [GAR]

WATSON, WILLIAM, in Rotterdam, a letter, 1705. [NRS.RH15.31.16]

WATT, JOHN, a young-man from Bo'ness, West Lothian, a seaman under Captain Aert Janszoon, testament, 12 April 1653, refers to Janet Brown, widow of Robert Clerk on the Schiedams dyke. [GAR.ONA.214.48.49]

WATT, PETER a Scot, was married in Bergen-op-Zoom, Brabant, on 2O December 1684. [WBA]

WATT, WILLIAM, a Scot, was married in Bergen-op-Zoom, Brabant, on 26 December 1732. [WBA]

WAUCHOP, JAMES, was granted a pass to travel from England to Holland on 21 September 1706. [TNA.SP44.393.91]

WEBSTER, JOHN, in Amsterdam, a letter, 1650. [NRS.GD406.1.2501]

WEBSTER, JOHN, from Errol, Perthshire, and Janet Millar from Dundee, were married in the Scots Kirk in Rotterdam on 6 July 1743. [GAR]

WEIR, JAMES, factor in Veere, Zealand,1641. [SHS.6/3]

WEIR, RICHARD, factor at Veere, Zealand, 1634, son of Thomas Weir a pewterer burgess of Edinburgh. [SHS.6/3]

WEMYSS, JAMES, a Scot, was married in Bergen op Zoom, Brabant, on 29 May 1621. [WBA]

WHITE, JANET, wife of John Walker, a Scottish innkeeper in Hellevoetsluys, testament, 7 November 1653, refers to John Gray a brewer's servant, and his wife Elisabeth Gordon in Bleijckers Alley, Rotterdam. [GAR.ONA.214.110.323]

WHYTE, ALEXANDER, son of Alexander Whyte in Glasgow, and Christian Murray widow of R. Fotheringham, were married in the Scots Kirk in Rotterdam on 4 January 1713. [GAR]

WIGHTMAN, ARCHIBALD, a merchant in Rotterdam, a deed, 1714. [NRS.RD2.103.2.412-418]

WIGHTMAN, ROBERT, from Edinburgh, was admitted as a citizen of Rotterdam on 20 March 1709. [GAR]

WILKIE, HENRY, of Bonnington, a merchant burgess of Edinburgh, was appointed Conservator of the Scots Privileges at Veere, Zealand, in 1671, he died on 8 April 1684. [SSN.220]

WILKIESON, THOMAS, a merchant in Amsterdam, 31 October 1725. [GAA.NA.]

WILLIAMS, ANDREW, from Leith, Midlothian, and Catelyntje Isaacs from Leiden, Holland, were married in Rotterdam on 17 December 1645. [GAR]

WILLIAMS, JOHN, from Aberdeen, and Marjory Hudson from Edinburgh, were married in Rotterdam on 31 March 1596. [GAR]

WILLIAMS, PETER, from Scotland, a seaman under Captain Aert Jans van Nes, testament, 6 March 1664, refers to James Hunter, a Scotsman, and his wife Catarijn Jans living in Jan Ariensgangh on the Schiedam dyke, and to his brother John and sister Janet and Margery in Linlithgow, West Lothian. [GAR.ONA.222.18.73]

'WILLIAMSDAUGHTER, HILLITGEN', a Scottish midwife, spouse to William Balfour a Scot, testament, 25 July 1639. [GAR.ONA.122.108.225]

WILLIAMSON, ALEXANDER, from Bo'ness, West Lothian, was admitted as a citizen of Rotterdam in 1740. [GAR]

WILLIAMSON, JOHN, from Edinburgh, and Maritgen Eemants from Rotterdam, were married in Rotterdam on 20 October 1602. [GAR]

WILLIAMSON, JOHN, in Rotterdam, was admitted as a burgess of Aberdeen on 23 August 1614. [ABR]

WILLIAMSON, JOHN, from Denny, Stirlingshire, and Adriana Perrius from Dordrecht, Holland, were married in the Scots Kirk in Rotterdam on 2 April 1739. [GAR]

WILSON, ANDREW, from Ayr, and Jailes Ritgers from Rotterdam, were married in Rotterdam on 13 October 1630. [GAR]

WILSON, ANDREW, from Lerwick in the Shetland Islands, was admitted as a citizen of Rotterdam in 1757. [GAR]

WILSON, E., a prisoner in Edinburgh Castle, petitioned to be released to go as a soldier to Holland in 1689. [NRS.GD226.9.222]

WILSON, HENRY, a Scotsman from Gouda, Holland, under Captain Haechswart, testament refers to his wife Maesdry Damster, 1 May 1630. [GAR.ONA.128.306.]

WILSON, JAMES, from Edinburgh, was admitted as a citizen of Rotterdam in 1738. [GAR]

WILSON, JOHN, from Glasgow, testament, 19 April 1633, refers to his half-brother James Williamson a broker burger of Rotterdam, also Richard Girling a skipper from Ipswich, England, and Dick Beton. [GAR.ONA.129.14.54]

WILSON, JOHN, from Bo'ness, West Lothian, was admitted as a citizen of Rotterdam on 21 November 1714. [GAR]

WILSON, JOHN, from Falkirk, Stirlingshire, and Jane Humphrey from Rotterdam, were married in the Scots Kirk in Rotterdam on 4 February 1739. [GAR], was admitted as a citizen of Rotterdam in 1741. [GAR]

WILSON, ROBERT, son of John Wilson in Edinburgh, and Jean Keith daughter of George Keith in Bo'ness, West Lothian, were married in the Scots Kirk in Rotterdam on 17 October 1701. [GAR]

WILSON, THOMAS, son of John Wilson in Wigtown, and Janet Turnbull widow of Edward Hume, were married in the Scots Kirk in Rotterdam on 20 September 1726. [GAR]

WILSON, THOMAS, son of John Wilsin in Carriden, West Lothian, and Mary Keir, daughter of Robert Keir in Rotterdam, were married in the Scots Kirk in Rotterdam on 6 May 1717. [GAR]

WILSON, WILLIAM, from Moffat, Dumfries-shire, was admitted as a citizen of Rotterdam in 1721. [GAR]

WILSON, WILLIAM, son of William Wilson in Buckhaven, Fife, and Janet Grant from Langside, Aberdeen, were married in the Scots Kirk in Rotterdam on 5 March 1778. [GAR]

WILSON, WILLIAM, son of Thomas Wilson a writer in Edinburgh, died in Surinam on 6 August 1812. [SM.74.886]

WILTON, JAMES, from Edinburgh, and Maria Philips from Rotterdam, were married in Rotterdam on 17 May 1676. [GAR]

WISHART, JAMES, of Logie, Scotland, in Holland, 1694. [NRS.CS96/1726/62]

WITCOMBE, WILLIAM, from Scotland, was admitted as a citizen of Rotterdam in 1770. [GAR]

WOOD, JOHN, from Glasgow, a young Scottish soldier aboard the New Rotterdam, master Jocchum Claeszoon, bound for the East Indies, testament, 27 March 1657, refers to William Williamson a Scotsman and his wife Maddeleentge Abramsdochter living in Glashaven. [GAR.ONA.216.59.221]

WRICHTEN, THOMAS, from Aberdeen, a cramer who was admitted as a burgess of Antwerpen, Flanders, in 1544. [SAA]

WRIGHT, ART PATERSON, from Bo'ness, West Lothian, and Grysella Joris from Rotterdam, were married in Rotterdam n 9 June 1686. [GAR]

WRIGHT, EDWARD, from Cromarty, Easter Ross, was admitted as a citizen of Rotterdam in 1734. [GAR]

WRIGHT, JOHN, from Falkirk, Stirlingshire, and Margaret Horn from Airth, Stirlingshire, were married in the Scots Kirk in Rotterdam on 6 December 1738. [GAR]

WYLLIE, ANDREW, a Scot, was married in Bergen-op-Zoom, Brabant, on 14 April 1700. [WBA]

WYNGART, JOHN, from Edinburgh, serving under Captain Hendricks, and Lysbeth Corsen widw of John Grim from London, were married in Rotterdam on 10 April 1594. [GAR]

WYTLING, MATTEUS, master of the Lydia Adriana van Amsterdam trading between Aberdeen and Rotterdam in 1749. [NRS.E504.1.3]

YAIR, JAMES, in Veere, Zealand, a letter, 1742. [NRS.GD18.5057]

YEATTS, ALEXANDER, from Aberdeen, was admitted as a citizen of Rotterdam in 1758. [GAR]

YOUNG, ABRAHAM, formerly a clothier in Leiden, Holland, teaching spinning in East Lothian, 1686. [NM#135]

YOUNG, ALEXANDER, from Leith, Midlothian, and Annetje Stockmans from Rotterdam, were married in Rotterdam on 9 August 1699. [GAR]

YOUNG, ANDREW, from Dunkeld, Perthshire, a seaman aboard the Little Holland under Captain Huijbrecht Jacobs, testament, 11 December 1665, refers to Robert William Sutherland a cobbler. [GAR.ONA.919.191.531]

YOUNG, GEORGE, eldest son of George Young a physician in Edinburgh, and Margaret Cassa, daughter of John Pierre Cassa in Leiden, Holland, who married in Colchester, England, 19 May 1671, parents of George Young, a declaratory of marriage, 1 September 1749. [NRS.CC8.6.230]

YOUNG, GILBERT, a Captain in General Murray's Regiment of Foot in the service of the States of Holland, husband of Elizabeth Dalziel, parents of Elizabeth, Gilbert, John and Thomas, a sasine, ca.1770. [NRS.RS23.XX.342]

YOUNG, WILLIAM, a Scot aboard the ship of Captain Bastiaen Aryenzoon Langaert, testament, 5 September 1625, refers to Jack Forsyth in Koestraet, Rotterdam. [GAR.ONA.128.57.147]

YOUNG, WILLIAM, from Ardrossan, and Helen daughter of Robert Taylor in Rotterdam, were married in the Scots Kirk in Rotterdam on 22 October 1755. [GAR]

YOUNGER, WALTER, from Bo'ness, West Lothian, and [1] Christian Roger, also from Bo'ness, were married in the Scots Kirk in Rotterdam on 22 December 1701, [2] Marjory J.ohnson widow of Ninian Johnson in the Canongate, Edinburgh on 21 January 1705. [GAR]

YOUNGER, WALTER, measurer at the Scottish Staple port of Veere, Zealand, a conveyance deed with Neil Brown a merchant in Venice, 1719. [NRS.RH11.2.1]

Some Shipping Links

Adventure of Perth, master John Stone, from Rotterdam to Perth in 1732. [NRS.CE52.4.1]

Alexander of Leith, master John Auchmutie, from Prestonpans to Holland, 1682. [NRS.E72.21.4]

Anna of Pittenweem, master John Aitchison, from Rotterdam to Leith in 1707. [NRS.GD29.427]

Bell of Montrose, master William Morrice, from Aberdeen to Veere, 1751. [NRS.E504.1.3]

Blessing of Aberdeen, master John Strachan, from Aberdeen to Veere, 1751. [with recruits for Colonel Stuart's regiment] [AJ.164]

Charles of Dundee, master James Gawen, from Rotterdam to Dundee, 1725. [NRS.CE70.1.1]

Christian of Kirkcaldy, master Alexander Simpson, from Kirkcaldy to Holland in 1682. [NRS.E72.9.13]

Christian of Bo'ness, master Duncan Glassford, to Rotterdam in 1707. [NRS.GD30.2214]

David of Wemyss, master James Gregorie, trading between Kirkcaldy and Holland 1680-1681. [NRS.E72.9/10/13]

Deskford of Portsoy, master David Rait, from Rotterdam to Aberdeen, 1750. [NRS.E504.1.3]

Enterprise of Aberdeen, from Aberdeen to Veere, 1787/1788/1789. [AJ.2080/2129/2181]

George of Leith, master John Bell, from Middelburg to Leith, 1690. [NRS.E72.15.44]

Good Intent, master John Henderson, from Rotterdam to Dundee, 1754. [NRS.CE70.1.3]

Good Intention of Dundee, master George Luggat, from Rotterdam to Dundee, 1726. [NRS.CE70.1.1]

Helen of Elphinstone, master James Garnock, from Aberdeen to Veere, 1749. [NRS.E504.1.3]

Janet of Kirkcaldy, master John Dougall, trading between Kirkcaldy and Holland in 1681-1682. [NRS.E72.9.10/13]

Janet of Kinghorn, master John Orrock, from Aberdeen to Rotterdam, 1750. [NRS.E504.1.3]

Lion of Leith, master John Acheson, from Leith to the Hook of Holland, 1685. [NRS.E72.15.34]

Lydia Adriana of Rotterdam, master Matteus Wytling, from Aberdeen to Rotterdam, 1749. [NRS.E504.1.3]

Margaret of Elie, master James Nairn, from Kirkcaldy to Bruges, 1682. [NRS.E72.9.12]

Margaret of Alloa, master George Fyffe, from Perth to Rotterdam, 1730. [NRS.CE52.1.3]

Margaret of Perth, master John Harrower, from Perth to Rotterdam, 1726. [NRS.CE52.4.1]

Marie of Pittenweem, master John Williamson, from Pittenweem to Bruges, 1684. [NRS.E72.9.17]

Owner's Goodwill of Perth, master John Young, from Perth to Rotterdam, 1762. [NRS.E504.27.5]

Peace of Elgin, master John Brodie, from Aberdeen to Veere, 1750. [NRS.E504.1.3]

Penelope of Dundee, master Alexander Ross, from Veere to Dundee, 1753. [NRS.CE70.1.3]

Prince Charles of Fraserburgh, master Alexander Steuart, from Rotterdam to Aberdeen, 1748. [NRS.E504.1.3]

Providentia of Christiansand, master Soren Lydersen, from Perth to Rotterdam, 1757. [NRS.E54.27.4]

Revenge of Aberdeen, master Walter Gordon, from Aberdeen to Veere, 1744. [NRS.E504.1.1]

Swift of Aberdeen, master William Spark, from Aberdeen to Veere and return in 1750. [NRS.E504.1.3]

Thomas and Elizabeth, master William Gillies, from Rotterdam to Dundee, 1724. [NRS.CE70.1.3]

Thomas and Mary of Peterhead, master James Wood, from Aberdeen to Rotterdam and return in 1749. [NRS.E504.1.3]

Three Brothers of Aberdeen, master Charles Leys, from Aberdeen to Veere and return in 1750. [NRS.E504.1.3]

Three Brothers of Poole, master William Leslie, from Rotterdam to Aberdeen, 1751. [NRS.E504.1.3]

Vernon of Aberdeen, master John Ferguson, from Aberdeen to Veee, 1744. [NRS.E504.1.1]

William of Dundee, master Morison, from Rotterdam to Dundee, 1725. [NRS.CE70.1.1]

Young Yeates of Friezland, master Hendrick Twitzes, from Aberdeen to Rotterdam, 1749. [NRS.E504.1.3]

..........**of Dordracht, [Dort], Holland,** master Steven 'Mithoing' and merchant Jaspar Janson, at Dundee, 7 April 1551. [Dundee Burgh Court Book, ii.47b]

.......**of Flushing, [Vlissengen], Zealand,** master Martyn Michaelson, from Aberdeen to Flushing, Zealand, in September 1558. [Aberdeen Burgh Records]

REFERENCES

ABR = Aberdeen Burgess Roll

AJ = Aberdeen Journal

BM = Blackwood's Magazine

CWF = Colonial Williamsburg Foundation

DPCA = Dundee, Perth, Cupar Advertiser

EA = Edinburgh Advertiser

EC = Edinburgh Correspondent

EEC = Edinburgh Evening Courant

GAA = Amsterdam Archives

GAB = Bergen-op-Zoom Archives

GAR = Rotterdam Archives

GAV = Veere Archives

GC = Glasgow Couier

MSC = Misc. Spalding Society, [Aberdeen, 1940]

NM = New Mills Cloth Manufactory, 1681-1793,

[Edinburgh, 1905]

NRAS= National Register of Archives in Scotland

NRS = National Records of Scotland, Edinburgh

RGSS= Register of the Great Seal of Scotland

SAA = S.A,Antwerpen, Poortersboeken

SM =   Scots Magazine

SSN =   The Scottish Staple in the Netherlands,

        [Den Haag, 1910]

SSV =   The Scottish Staple at Veere, [London, 1909]

WBA =   West Brabant Archives